As the biological mom in a stepfa of blending families. Stepmoms Kathi Lipp and Carol Boley write with honesty, grace, and humor, offering down-to-earth help for anyone in stepparenting roles. It's like having friends who have already scouted out the route to help you travel this often-difficult road. They totally get it.

—LINDA CARLBLOM
Author, *Bible Blessings for Bedtime; Interactive Children's Sermons: 52 Messages from the Psalms; Bailey and the Santa Fe Secret* (Camp Club Girls Book 15); *Bailey's Peoria Problem* (Camp Club Girls Book 6)

While I'm not a stepmom, I was the mom in a "step" household. I can only say that I wish we'd had this common sense and insightful advice when my husband and I were raising our family.

—PEGGY LEVESQUE
Author, *Ashes in the Wind*

I had assumed that my husband and I, with our combined five children, would be happy and have a lot of fun, like the Brady bunch! Well, that didn't happen. I wanted my husband's attention, but with five littles to care for, it was very much *not* a honeymoon! All I can say is that only by the grace of God did we all make it and survive and now all love each other unconditionally. This book would have been a great how-to book for me; believe me I did search the Christian bookstores!

—SYLVIA
Blended family for 37 years
Two mine, Three his, All ours

Kathi and Carol have great advice, great insight, and their ideas really work. For me Chapter 9, "At All Costs, Protect Your Marriage", was so right on! The kids will grow up and move out, and what's left is you looking at the man you fell in love with however number of years ago, the man who was with you through all the struggles, all the tears, all the sacrifices, all the good, the bad, and the ugly moments. And what an awesome example for your kids to see that a healthy and loving marriage can exist.

—CARRIE
Blended Family for 16 years
Four mine, One his, All ours

This book is a must have for every Christian stepmom! I only wish I'd had it 28 years ago when I married the "World's Greatest Fighter Pilot" and inherited beautiful 6-year-old and 8-year-old daughters. This well-researched and well-written book covers so many aspects of successful stepparenting. While the topics are often difficult, the delivery of the wise content is done with such humor that you find yourself navigating those turbulent waters with less drama. This book helps Christian stepmoms realize that they are part of a huge tribe of God lovers who love their spouses and kids and want to do stepparenting God's way.

—ELLIE KAY
"America's Financial Expert"® and "America's Military Family Expert"™
International speaker and best-selling author of 15 books, including *Heroes at Home* and *Lean Body, Fat Wallet*
Mother of seven, including two stepdaughters

but I'm not a WICKED STEPMOTHER!

Secrets of Successful Blended Families

FOCUS
IN THE
FAMILY

KATHI LIPP & CAROL BOLEY

but I'm not a wicked stepmother!

Secrets of Successful Blended Families

TYNDALE HOUSE PUBLISHERS, INC.
CAROL STREAM, ILLINOIS

But I'm Not a Wicked Stepmother!

Copyright © 2015 by Kathi Lipp and Carol Boley

A Focus on the Family book published by
Tyndale House Publishers, Inc., Carol Stream, Illinois 60188

Focus on the Family and the accompanying logo and design are federally registered trademarks of Focus on the Family, 8605 Explorer Drive, Colorado Springs, CO 80920.

TYNDALE and Tyndale's quill logo are registered trademarks of Tyndale House Publishers, Inc.

All Scripture quotations, unless otherwise indicated, are taken from *the Holy Bible, New International Version*®. NIV®. Copyright © 1973, 1978, 1984 by Biblica, Inc.™ Used by permission of Zondervan. All rights reserved worldwide (www.zondervan.com). Scripture quotations marked (NASB) are taken from the *New American Standard Bible*®. Copyright © 1960, 1962, 1963, 1968, 1971, 1972, 1973, 1975, 1977, 1995 by The Lockman Foundation. Used by permission. (www.Lockman.org). Scripture quotations marked (NKJV) are taken from the *New King James Version*®. Copyright © 1982 by Thomas Nelson, Inc. Used by permission. All rights reserved.

The use of material from or references to various websites does not imply endorsement of those sites in their entirety. Availability of websites and pages is subject to change without notice.

All stories in this book are true and are used by permission. In some cases, people's names and certain details of their stories have been changed to protect the privacy of the individuals involved. However, the facts of what happened and the underlying principles have been conveyed as accurately as possible.

Editor: Brandy Bruce
Cover photograph of mudroom, copyright © Ian Nolan / Getty Images. All rights reserved.
Cover photograph of broom, copyright © Sitade / Getty Images. All rights reserved.
Cover photograph of ribbon, copyright © mizar_21984 / DollarPhotoClub. All rights reserved.

Cataloging-in-Publication Data is available through the Library of Congress.

ISBN: 978-1-58997-801-0

Printed in the United States of America
1   2   3   4   5   6   7   8   9/20   19   18   17   16   15

Dedicated to my sister-in-love Debbie Lipp,
and my friend Michele Cushatt.
Two of the bravest, smartest, and most loving stepmoms I know.
You've taught me well.
And in loving memory of Mary Jane Lipp.
Roger and I could not have asked for a more loving
and accepting stepmom.
Your legacy will be felt for generations to come.
—*Kathi*

This book is dedicated to my family—Jim,
Abby, Allison, and Andrea Boley.
You are each the answer to my prayers,
and I love you with my whole heart.
—*Carol*

CONTENTS

FOREWORD

"Now we're going to be a big, happy family."

He smiled as he said it, his face turned up toward mine. We stood just outside the broad double doors of the Castle Pines country club. Me, a fresh, young bride dressed in ivory lace. Him, a nine-year-old boy sporting grass-stained khakis, white button-down shirt, clip-on tie, and tennis shoes. My new stepson.

Hours before, I'd stood inches from his dad, our hands and fingers interlaced, and exchanged promises of loving, honoring, and cherishing. Now, after a fairy-tale ceremony, a sit-down reception, and hours of dancing like Cinderella and the prince at her ball, we gathered our things—and our collective three young boys—to head home. It was time to start a new life together. A brand spankin' new family of five.

That's when my newly acquired nine-year-old made his happy-family pronouncement. And I very nearly cried.

Holy happily ever after. Thank You, Jesus.

If only his pronouncement had been prophetic. On the contrary, it took mere weeks for the mirage of "happy family" to be replaced by the reality of stepfamily life. Dreamy? Hardly. More nightmarish. Our new family scenario involved things like conflicting parenting styles, threatened ex-spouses, role confusion, power struggles, alternating homes and parenting schedules, and custody battles. Not to mention disappointment. Truckloads of disappointment. This wasn't at all the family I'd dreamed of.

Perhaps my greatest disappointment came in the form of my two less-than-enthusiastic stepsons. Sure, they seemed happy enough through our wedding day. But once we moved my four-year-old and me into their territory, and they felt conflicting loyalties, everything changed. No longer was I the welcomed mother figure. Instead, I became the unwanted imposter. The reason for all stepsons' woes. The root of all their unhappiness. The cause of all our familial struggles. THE STEPMOTHER. [Insert evil orchestra music here.]

After spending a lifetime dreaming of motherhood, I now found stepmotherhood to be something different altogether. And far beyond my skill set. I felt somewhat comfortable when it came to mothering my four-year-old. But as for these precious, two stepsons who seemed bent on making me earn my keep, I didn't have a clue. What was my role exactly? Why did I always feel unwanted in my own home? When would we start to bond like a real family? And would my stepsons ever learn to love me?

Tough questions, every one. Without answers, I stumbled my way through, learning by trial and error. But mostly error.

It's now been fourteen years since my husband and I said, "I do." Our boys are grown, and I'm happy to report we all love each other. Truly. We're not a perfect family, and we still have moments of struggle. But we pushed through, and by a miracle of God, we came out the other side stronger, better, and a *family.*

Looking back, however, I see a trail of heartache that could've been avoided, at least in part. The truth is, I could've used a friend during those early years, when my naive enthusiasm was severely dashed. Whether it was my sense of independence or my shame at the stepmom label, I isolated myself. And I didn't have to. Now, on the other side, I know the entire process could have been far less painful and— dare I say it?—enjoyable if I'd had a friend, a fellow stepmom, walking me through it. There's nothing more soothing and hope infusing than someone who's been there and made it out alive.

Enter Kathi Lipp—mom, stepmom, Jesus lover, maker of mistakes, and learner of tough lessons—and her partner in crime, Carol Boley. When it comes to stepmothering, these women have "been there, done that" and lived to tell the story. Through these pages, they will certainly pass along some valuable lessons and practical advice. Take notes, talk about it all with a friend, give their ideas a whirl and see if they work. But more than the how-tos, by the time you read the last page, you will know you're not alone.

We're in this together, my friend. For better or worse, adults and children alike. And from where I sit, building your stepfamily is not only possible. It's worth it.

Cheering for you,

Michele Cushatt

Speaker and author of *Undone: A Story of Making Peace with an Imperfect Life*

www.michelecushatt.com

Introduction

I will be glad and rejoice in your love, for you saw

my affliction and knew the anguish of my soul....

Praise be to the LORD, for he showed his wonderful

love to me when I was in a besieged city.

—PSALM 31:7, 21

Kathi and Carol

Welcome to the club.

Oh, I (Kathi) know it's a club you never dreamed of joining. Really, what little girl writes in her journal, "Dear Diary, when I grow up, I want to be a stepmom"?

No one. Ever.

But at some point you did the same thing I did. You fell in love. (Silly girl!)

You fell in love with this amazing man who had everything you were looking for: He was kind and strong, smart and funny. He was a leader, and he adored you. Oh, and he had a bonus: children.

Wrapped up with this amazing man was the bonus of kids.

Yes. People tried to warn you ...

"Being a stepmom is the hardest thing you will ever do."

"Oh, the ex is going to drive you crazy."

"My stepkids didn't even like me until they were adults."

You heard all the warnings. But if you were anything like me, you assumed that those warnings just wouldn't apply to you.

I figured that we would be the exception—because my husband and I really loved each other. And we loved God. And doesn't love conquer all? And we were not afraid of some hard work and a little therapy thrown in for good measure. And I get along with most of the people in my life. Oh, sure, there are a few people who wouldn't sign up for the Kathi Fan Club, but getting along with people? That's my specialty. If we just love each other enough and love the kids enough and work hard and get some therapy, that will take care of 80 percent of our problems, right?

If you're already part of the club, at this point you're thinking, *Oh, you poor, naive, silly girl.* Because there are things you only truly understand when you've been part of the Stepmoms Club for a while. Here are a few of the things I didn't understand until later:

- You, who have never been jealous a day in your life, will need to deal with envy on several fronts. You may not only be envious of the time your husband spends with his kids (remember, there is no honeymoon period for the blended family), but you may be dealing with jealousy regarding his ex-wife as well. (Oh, and let's talk about being jealous of your friends' families, which aren't so complex.)
- Everything is more complicated in a blended family. From school forms to wedding days, there is a whole cast of characters to be dealt with, as well as feelings and expectations to manage as you work to keep the peace.
- Your assumption that if you're nice and respectful to your stepkids, his ex-wife, and her family, they will be nice back is blown out of the water.
- Your assumption that you will *want* to be nice and respectful all the time is also not a reality.

I went into my marriage with Roger assuming the best about all the parties involved. But here's the thing: Being part of a blended family messes with everyone.

I'm sure your husband's ex is beloved at work and cherished in her family.

Your stepkids are adored by the neighbors and loved at school.

His ex-wife's family members are model citizens and have a rich circle of friends at their church.

Oh, and you and your husband? Just a whole bunch of awesome.

But then you take all these hurting people and announce to them, "Even though you are all in pain, even though you aren't very fond of each other and, in fact, may even hate each other on occasion, now you have to make a family." Blending a family takes those frayed threads we're all running around with and pulls on the very fabric of who we are. It causes us to feel weak and vulnerable and act in ways that we never thought we would. Trust me. I know.

One day early in our marriage, Roger received an e-mail from his ex-wife that was pretty awful. (She and I like each other now, but we both had a lot of things to work out, especially early in our relationship.) Roger and I sat down and responded in a very thoughtful, measured way.

I was so proud of the way I handled it that I actually jumped on my blog and wrote a little article on how to handle a difficult e-mail. I was pretty proud of myself for having so much grace in such a tough circumstance.

A little while later, Roger's ex sent another e-mail accusing my husband of not putting their kids' best interests at the top of the list in our house.

That's when I lost my mind.

I fired back an e-mail filled with vile words (and maybe without my husband actually approving it), letting her know that it was none of her business. I listed all the ways we desperately cared for her kids, and the sacrifices we made.

Have I ever sent an e-mail like that to anyone else in my life? Not a chance.

Do I still get upset when I remember that story and how her attacks on our parenting and character made me feel? Absolutely.

Was I totally in the wrong for how I responded? Yep.

As I said, I'm a nice person. But there's something about these step-situations that makes a sane person act in some not-so-sane ways.

So, my friend, welcome to the club. Other adults may not understand. You may feel a constant mix of pain and guilt, and every once in a while, a teaspoon of hope gets thrown in. I know you signed up for the role of stepmom, but I'm guessing you truly had no idea what you were getting into. None of us did.

So in this book, Carol and I want to encourage you, though we know it may feel as though there isn't a lot of encouragement to be had sometimes. We also want to recognize that this stepmom thing is hard, but there are some wonderful rewards in it—not just what God can do *with* you in your role as stepmom to build up your husband's kids, but also what God can do *in* you to help you become more like Him.

When I (Carol) joined the ranks of stepmothers more than thirty years ago as a never-married thirty-something with no children marrying a widower with a five-year-old daughter, nothing had prepared me for the daily realities of the job. The only role models I could find were in fairy tales and were always described as "wicked." I knew I was *not* a "wicked stepmother"; I certainly knew I wasn't living in a fairy tale; and I also knew I needed help in a hurry.

I searched Scripture, interviewed pastors and family counselors, and compared experiences with dozens of others helping rear their spouses' children. I learned that even though it can be rewarding, the role of stepmother can also be draining and demanding. "Being a step-mom is harder than biological parenting, and the delights are fewer," one stepmother told me. "I have all the demands of parenting but none of the power."

So how does a stepmother cope? And how do Christian women apply the grace of Jesus Christ to the hard work of stepparenting?

Here's what I discovered. According to the Stepfamily Foundation, second marriages only stand a 40 percent chance of survival, and third marriages less than that. Kathi and I want to improve not only your chances of survival as a stepmother but also your enjoyment of and satisfaction in the role. We hope to do that through our love and care for you expressed in this book.

And I have a confession. After more than thirty years of compar-ing notes with other stepmothers, I discovered that I have had the easiest circumstances of any stepmother I know or have ever heard of—something I suspected all along. Over the years I have listened to stepmothers share their stories of conflict, abuse, guilt, and shame. I have wept with them and have also felt like the sole survivor of a plane crash—grateful to have survived, yet feeling strangely guilty.

You have it easy. Your trials are nothing compared to hers! I have told myself while listening to stepmothers tell their horror stories, and they have agreed with me! I have a loving, supportive husband who values our relationship, second only to his relationship with God; a nurturing faith community; and a stepdaughter whom I love and who loves me.

But it hasn't come easy. I still remember the confusion of those early days, the frustration, and the fear. I remember.

And I've learned a lot along the way. So has Kathi. We've learned a few things that we believe can help you on your stepmother journey. The fact is that we all struggle. We all need help. We all need to for-give and be forgiven. We all face common issues and fears. And we all want to know what it means—and what it takes—to be a successful stepmother.

You're not alone in your journey. Approximately hundreds of new stepfamilies are created every day.[1] Sadly, according to statistics, close to 60 percent of those marriages will fail,[2] often, in part, because of the strain of raising stepchildren. Christians are not immune from these staggering statistics. *Kathi and I do not want to be, nor do we want you to be, one of those statistics.*

For whatever reason, for far too long the church has sidestepped the reality of stepfamilies in our midst and the needs of stepmothers, in particular (but that's another book!). It's time for us to accept reality, grow up, and speak the truth in love to one another. And have as much fun as we can along the way!

In 1989 I wrote an article for Focus on the Family titled, "When You're Mom No. 2," which struck a nerve with stepmothers. It was later included as a chapter in *The Focus on the Family Guide to Growing a Healthy Home*, under the section titled, "Focus on Difficult Family Problems." The article was reprinted by mental-health clinics, crisis pregnancy centers, churches, and counselors in the United States and internationally. I gave radio interviews on both local and national shows and received letters from stepmothers seeking advice. As a result, I realized what a need there was and is for help and hope for stepmoms.

In the twenty-five years since, in addition to my other writing and speaking, I have continued my research and interviews, speaking with and counseling stepmoms who have asked me to "please write a book"—*this* book. When I met Kathi, I recognized a kindred spirit, someone who shares my love of God, His people, and writing and speaking to help connect the two. I loved her spirit, her joy, her humor, her openness, her warmth, and her kindness. Upon getting to know her better and hearing her stories about her blended family, I remember thinking, *She gets it!* I knew we would make a great team, and I was thrilled when she agreed that we should write this book together.

Today Kathi and I wish we could sit across the kitchen table from you with a cup of coffee and really talk. We know *we* would love it; we would like to know your personal story, to hear your challenges, surprises, and victories as a stepmother and to share ours with you.

Yet even without meeting you, we think we know a few things about you. Do any of the following feelings, so common to stepmothers, sound familiar?

- You're exhausted—not just physically but emotionally— from struggling to succeed in a job no one sets as a life goal.
- You're confused and angry as a result of trying to understand the entangled relationships of stepfamily life and feeling like your needs are secondary to those of everyone else in your stepfamily. At times you feel used.
- You're lonely and frustrated from being the outsider, not knowing the established routines, traditions, and inside jokes in your own family.
- You feel guilty and depressed for not instantly feeling love for your stepchildren, who sometimes act as your adversaries, deliberately setting out to undermine your marriage.
- You're discouraged and disillusioned—the reality of your stepfamily life is neither what you expected nor wanted. And yet you remain hopeful.

We know one more thing about you. We applaud the fact that you *care* about being a good stepmother. The fact that you would even consider accepting a job of this enormity, caring for someone else's children, makes you someone we want to know.

This is hard work—the hardest work most of us will ever do. Dr. Phil McGraw agrees. In *Family First*, he writes, "There's no doubt that being a stepparent is one of the most difficult roles any adult will ever assume."[3]

Dr. James Dobson, founder of Focus on the Family, writes, "It is possible to blend families successfully, and millions have done it. But the task is difficult, and you will need help pulling it off."[4]

We all know firsthand that stepfamilies are far more complicated than traditional families and that parenting stepchildren differs in many aspects from rearing natural, adopted, or foster children. We have had to define our roles, our relationships, and the rules of it all, making them up as we go along.

Perhaps hardest of all, we have had neither a realistic way to measure our success nor many guidelines to get there. Most stepmothers told me they didn't consider themselves success stories. Why? Because their relationships with their stepchildren weren't all they wanted them to be, even though they had done many of the right things to build strong relationships.

You may feel the same way. But I have good news for you: Your success does not depend on the outcome of your stepmothering efforts. Your success depends only on those things *you can control*—your attitudes, words, and actions (including the choice to accept God's grace and love). Your success as a stepmother does not—indeed, *cannot*—depend on those things *you can't control*, including the actions of your stepchildren. You can be a successful stepmother regardless of how they think, act, or speak. If stepchildren do turn out well and you have a good relationship with them, you can consider that an added bonus.

What a relief to know our success as stepmothers depends on believing that God loves us, and that by His grace, He will enable us to love others even when it seems impossible. Remember, love is not just gushy feelings. The role of stepmother demands strength of character, endurance, resilience, wisdom, flexibility, a willingness to serve and sacrifice, an ability to love unconditionally, and a constant reliance on God. It also requires a commitment to put the needs of others (even people you may not like and who may not like you) ahead of your own, with no expectation of appreciation from anyone. (Doesn't this sound like a description of Jesus?)

Accepting this reality and working within this framework may seem like too high a price to pay, and certainly more than you bargained for when you signed the marriage license. Keep this thought in mind, however: Many Christian stepmothers, even those struggling in the toughest circumstances, find that their deepening friendship with God, resulting from staying humbly on their knees before Him, is *more than worth the pain.* Stepmotherhood can be just the instrument God uses to mold us into the image of Christ.

One of the greatest needs of stepmothers is someone to talk with openly and freely who empathizes and listens without judging. We need someone who has fought in the same trenches, who understands the unique trials and relates to the same heartaches. We want to hear from other stepmothers; we want to know what has worked for them in this most challenging of roles.

There is nothing you could say that would shock me or make me think less of you—something I suspect only another stepmother could say. (You were tempted to put rat poison in your stepchild's food? I've heard that one before, and I know you didn't really mean it. Or maybe you *did* mean it, but you controlled yourself. Or maybe you acted on a similar temptation, and now you suffer from guilt and condemnation.) Whatever your situation, there's hope for you.

Stepmothering is such a complicated role that no one book can cover all the aspects. Some of the tips stepmothers share aren't easily categorized but spill into more than one area of life. What follows is short (Kathi and I know how busy you are), practical, helpful, encouraging advice that you can apply immediately.

Please think of this book as the next best thing to a support group of stepmothers, plus some pastors and counselors, sitting around that kitchen table. Is the coffee ready?

I doubt if many of us stepmoms would dare to call ourselves experts, but we are all experienced. I personally relate to C. S. Lewis, who wrote, "Think of me as a fellow-patient in the same hospital who, having been admitted a little earlier, [could] give some advice."[5] As you read this book, you will receive advice from those who understand and share your situation.

The practical, tried-and-true techniques presented in the following chapters have helped other stepmothers just like you. They tell how stepmothers let God help and teach them in their roles, just as He will do for you. The advice in this book shows what the two great commandments of Jesus—loving God and loving people—look like when lived out by stepmothers. Even more important, it shows how God's grace makes stepmothering well possible.

This is the book I wish I'd had when I became a stepmother—one that offers understanding, support, encouragement, guidance, and some humor from successful stepmothers who have "been there, done that" and who want desperately, as you do, to prosper in their roles, for the good of their families and the glory of God. Try the ideas. They work. You will find you are among friends.

Some of this information may be new to you. Some of it may be a reminder and reinforcement of what you know to be true. Take it and use it to best suit your needs. And if something doesn't seem like a practical point for you now, accept what *does* apply and save the rest for later, share it with a friend, or just blow it gently away. If you aren't a Christian, please don't let that keep you from reading further. There is love and success in this book for you.

Please read this book with love, for that's how it was written, from these stepmothers' hearts to yours.

ONE

God's Plan for Stepmoms

Have I not commanded you? Be strong

and courageous. Do not be terrified; do

not be discouraged, for the LORD your God

will be with you wherever you go.

—JOSHUA 1:9

Carol

I remember the time (And how can I not? My family never lets me forget!) when my best intentions and eagerness to please my family backfired, resulting in an epic fail. I was still adjusting to being the stay-at-home mom of a six-year-old. Before I married Jim, I had been neither stay at home nor a mom. Part of my new role included planning and preparing dinner for people who wanted it *every night*. One afternoon, thinking I'd better decide on something for supper, I surveyed the contents of our fridge and pantry. My family loved any kind of Mexican food, so the ground beef, salsa, cheese, and refried beans sounded like the makings of a delicious Mexican casserole.

Abby was eager to help. "Will you get out the tortilla chips, please?" I asked. She couldn't find any in the pantry. Really? They were a staple in our house. I went over to double-check. Yep. She was right.

I stood staring into the pantry, as if that would cause tortilla chips to mysteriously materialize, and spotted what looked like the perfect solution.

Soon after Jim got home, we all sat down to eat. Everything went well . . . until the first bite. Jim, usually so complimentary, didn't say a word. Abby wrinkled her nose. Jim looked at her, sympathy in his eyes, and shook his head ever so slightly as a warning not to say anything and just eat it.

They seemed to fill up much sooner than usual and wanted dessert almost immediately.

After clearing the table, Jim hugged me and said, "Thanks for dinner, darling."

"You're welcome," I answered, pleased with myself. "I tried a little experiment. What did you think of the casserole?"

"Um, it tasted a little . . . *different* tonight."

I quizzed him on the mystery ingredient. "Something salty. Something chip-like. Something delicious. Want to guess?" He couldn't even imagine. I felt such pride as I proclaimed, "Wheat Thins!" Jim just stared at me, unable to speak.

Apparently my family *didn't* love any kind of Mexican food. *What?* They especially didn't love Mexican food made with Wheat Thins. I learned they're picky that way.

I've also learned that some things are so good, there's just no substitute for them.

That story not only reminds me of all the adjustments of our early days as a blended family; it also illustrates for me God's plan for stepmoms. Knowing I am loved, I can risk doing my best for my family, and whenever I fail, there is grace to cover me. And there's grace to cover you. Grace. It's God's plan for stepmoms. There's just no substitute for it.

But how do we receive grace for our own lives and share it with others? Some of us need help with that. Just ask Joyce.

"My biggest frustration is not finding anybody who admits that her stepfamily is not 'one big, happy family,'" Joyce lamented. "I think they are either in denial or lying, but it makes it so difficult to talk to anyone about my problems. I need a stepmother mentor."

Joyce is right. It *is* hard to find a stepmother who will honestly discuss her struggles and challenges. Fear of being judged and rejected keeps many stepmothers from speaking truthfully about their feelings and circumstances. You, too? We wonder how we can share our problems and concerns, speaking the truth in love about our husbands, their ex-wives, our ex-husbands, our kids, and our stepchildren without sounding critical, judgmental, or downright *wicked*. Sometimes it feels as if we, as stepmoms, aren't allowed to say the same things some biological moms say.

"If they're all alive at the end of the day, then I did my job!" a biological mom can say, and everyone laughs. Let a stepmom say the same thing, except to another stepmother, and eyebrows shoot up.

It's also difficult to describe just how frustrating and challenging the job can actually be. Nobody but another stepmom gets it. Stepmother mentors *are* hard to come by. But God's plan for us is not to be alone and isolated. Part of our prayer for this book is that it will open up conversation between stepmoms and provide a community where we can be safe to express our feelings, receive support and encouragement, shed the shame, and know we belong. A place where we aren't outsiders.

I want to know others have walked this path before me. I want to know how they did it. I want to know I'm not alone. Thinking perhaps the Bible provided a "good stepmother" model, I searched Scripture for someone with whom to identify. Thankfully I found someone who also stood in unfamiliar, hostile territory. I found someone who faced circumstances that threatened to take down not only a family but a nation. I found someone else who also inherited the fearful position of leadership. I found Joshua.

It may seem odd to use a man as a model stepmother, but stick with me. He provides us with a powerful example.

Scripture records that "after the death of Moses . . . the LORD said to Joshua son of Nun, Moses' aide: 'Moses my servant is dead. Now then, you and all these people, get ready to cross the Jordan River into the land I am about to give to them'" (Joshua 1:1–2).

Joshua, Moses is dead! Big changes in your life require major adjustments. Be brave.

Stepmom, these children are now part of your world. Big changes in your life require major adjustments. Be brave.

Take these people and cross the Jordan River. I will be with you.

Take these people and make a stepfamily. I will be with you.

Those are encouraging words. God knew that if Joshua focused on his circumstances, they would overwhelm him. God wanted Joshua to focus on the fact that God was with him, and that fact guaranteed Joshua's victory. God wants us to know the same thing is true for us as well.

Challenges threatened to discourage Joshua, yet he obeyed God's command to step out in faith, crossing the Jordan River into enemy territory, ironically called the Promised Land.

Accepting reality and acting in spite of our fears is part of our job description too. The theme of ordinary, flawed human beings overcoming great odds because God is with them echoes throughout the pages of Scripture—and now it's our turn. If there were a Hebrews 11:41, that's where our names would fall. A verse could read, "By faith (your name here) served her family, facing challenges with grace and courage. She showed them the love of Christ, and the joy of the Lord was her strength."

We also stand, like Joshua, on the bank of a Jordan River we must cross. Panic threatens to paralyze us, but God tells us to get going. As stepmothers we begin our journey across the Jordan by embracing the reality of our circumstances—not denying or wishing them away—and acting with courage.

But how do we act courageously when we don't feel brave? Like Joshua, we remember that God is with us, and He will supply everything we need (Philippians 4:19). He is the brave One. He is delighted to share His courage with us when we ask. Our job is to receive what He supplies, including courage.

It's a formidable thing to step into the lives of someone else's children. We wonder in what moment of madness we thought we could manage this job, and at times we're not even sure we want to.

But God doesn't want us living in discouragement, depression, or distress. His plan for stepmothers involves living lives of fulfillment, contentment, and joy. And in His grace, He shows us how—often *in spite of* our circumstances and current relationship status.

In the New Testament story of Mary and Martha, while Martha was "distracted by all the preparations that had to be made," busy being "worried and upset about many things," Jesus reminded her—and He reminds us—that "only one thing is needed" (Luke 10:40, 41–42). I love that Jesus didn't condemn Martha for her service to Him. Instead, He gently pointed out that, in her service, she was worried about *many things* because she didn't first do the *one thing* He considered necessary, the *one thing* that her sister Mary had chosen to do—sit "at the Lord's feet listening to what he said" (verse 39).

Only one thing is necessary? we wonder. As stepmoms we face dozens of demands. How can there be only one thing?

Because God knows how to take care of us. And when we sit at His feet and listen to Jesus, we receive from Him wisdom, guidance, and self-control. He enables us to serve Him and others with joy, without worrying and growing overly upset, even when others complain about us. God's design for us as stepmothers begins with "one thing"—to sit at His feet and receive from Him all He delights in supplying us to live the abundant life, a life characterized by peace and joy in spite of our circumstances.

As a stepmom, you know "the rule" is to love your stepkids. Jesus will show you how when you sit at His feet and listen to Him. He will prompt you with just the right words to say, or He'll clamp a hand over your mouth. He is a good Shepherd.

When Abby was in junior high, we carpooled with neighbors to her school, twenty minutes away. I appreciated those mornings, especially in the winter, when our neighbors drove and I could let my other daughters, Andrea and Allison, ages one and five, stay in their pj's a little longer.

One morning I met Abby at the kitchen door to say good-bye when her ride drove up.

"Got your coat?" I asked.

"No, I won't need it," she answered.

"It's supposed to be the coldest day of the year," I said. "Better get it."

She marched back to her room, returning a few minutes later with a wad of denim slung across her shoulders. Only it wasn't her jacket; it was a pair of overalls. She had seen the denim in a pile on her bedroom floor and grabbed it. Now she had to return to her room *a second time* to get her coat, and she was irritated with me for *not wanting her to freeze to death.* The carpool driver started to honk, which added to my list of frustrations. This situation had the potential to go very wrong.

If I snapped at Abby, I would send her off to school angry and frustrated, wearing her bad mood like I hoped she would wear that jacket. That wasn't what I wanted. Irritation would hang between us like a fog all day until we could talk again when she returned home. That *certainly* wasn't what I wanted. It would poison the atmosphere in the carpool. I glanced at Allison and Andrea and saw two little girls in footy pajamas watching to see what their mommy would do.

And here came Abby, likely wondering the same thing. I gave her a smile and a hug when she returned from her room with her *actual denim jacket*; and then I said good-bye with my usual send-off: "I pray for Jesus to bless your day." And I meant it.

I turned and smiled at Allison and Andrea. They smiled back. Crisis averted. Thank You, Jesus. And when I thought about it, it *was* kind of funny, in a junior high kind of way. Looking back, perhaps I shouldn't have made Abby go back for the coat. If she had gotten cold enough that day, maybe she wouldn't need a reminder from me the next time the temperature dropped. Or maybe she really didn't need her jacket. People have different thermostats. And just because she took the coat didn't mean she actually wore it.

Nonetheless, sitting at Jesus' feet "listening to what he said" earlier that morning, before anyone else was up, had enabled me to control myself. And thank goodness there was grace for those other times when, sadly, I didn't.

When we face challenges that threaten to overwhelm us, God gives us the strength to persevere, trusting Him for the outcome. He knows we need specific instruction, so, thankfully, He gives us the formula for success in His words to Joshua:

1. *Accept reality.* "Moses my servant is dead" (Joshua 1:2). Life is hard, full of trouble, pain, and sorrow. Your stepfamily has been born of loss, either through death or divorce. Everyone has suffered. We know that.

2. *Prepare for action.* "Get ready to cross the Jordan River" (verse 2). Prepare for action. Get organized and make a plan. Kathi and I are here to help.

3. *Know that you are not alone.* "I will be with you" (verse 5). God and all of His resources are available to you; therefore, you can succeed. It's important to believe this.

4. *Stand firm.* "Be strong and courageous. . . . Be strong and very courageous" (verses 6, 7). It will be tough, but stay

faithful to your task. Do the right thing, even when you don't feel like it. God will supply what you need to accomplish this.

5. *Know God's heart.* "Be careful to obey all the law . . . do not turn from it to the right or to the left, *that you may be successful wherever you go*" (verse 7, emphasis added). Study God's Word, making it the basis for your thoughts, words, attitudes, and actions. This is what it means to be successful. This is the "one thing" Jesus considers necessary. Everything else flows from this.

In other words, "Stepmother, don't panic; stay focused on God and His Book of Instructions. You will need them. Remember, God is greater than your problems, and He will navigate you through them. Focus on Him, who is the answer to your problems, rather than on the problems themselves. This is the key to your success."

Scripture doesn't record it, but I wonder whether Joshua ever felt unappreciated, unpopular, and not the *real* leader because he wasn't the first to hold the position. (Sound familiar, stepmother?) Some of those stubborn Israelites probably resented Joshua's leadership because he wasn't Moses.

Do you feel inferior because you aren't your husband's first wife or his children's first—and only—mother figure? Many a stepmom tortures herself needlessly with comparisons to an ex-wife or her stepchildren's biological mother. Please don't.

Do you think some of the Israelites esteemed Moses more in death than during his life and forgot that they had openly rebelled against his leadership and authority?

Children often view their mother idealistically, even if she abandoned or abused them, *simply because she is their mother*. In their eyes, a stepmother *never* measures up, *simply because she is their stepmother*, and understandably so; we all know mothers are unique and irreplaceable.

But stepmothers aren't here to replace anybody. God made us with our own individual characteristics. We each bring God-given strengths into our stepfamilies. God wants us to do *our* part, not anyone else's, knowing He is with us. We hope that our stepchildren will come to appreciate us for who we are and the role we play in their lives, and they certainly may. But there is no guarantee. While each stepmother's "part" may look different from another's based on individual family circumstances, each one of us has received her marching orders, and like Joshua's, they are daunting.

Our job, like that of both Moses and Joshua, centers on loving God and obeying Him, relying on His love and grace for us, and acting on His assurance that He is able to provide for us everything we need to succeed.

A big part of loving God involves loving others, even when it isn't easy. Just as God was with Joshua, He is with us, and He enables us to do what looks and feels impossible. In this book, we'll discover what that looks like for stepmothers. Like Joshua, we may be second (or third), but that doesn't make us second best, second choice, or second class.

We can be stepmothers who honor God and serve our families successfully (regardless of their response) because He is with us and will enable us as we first, like Mary, sit "at the Lord's feet listening to what he said" (Luke 10:39) and then step out in faith and obedience.

I discovered that neither Moses nor Joshua asked God for his job; in fact, Moses tried to talk his way out of it! I suspect you never set out to become a stepmother; you never considered it a life goal. I have met no one who said her dream was to one day become a stepmother. Yet here we are!

When the angel of the Lord showed up before Joshua's big battle, he told Joshua that he was there not to take sides but to take over (Joshua 5:13–14). In order to succeed as stepmothers, we need the Lord to take over our "battle plans" as well. Perhaps with pounding hearts and courage we don't feel yet, we say, like Joshua, "I accept the reality of my life. I face forbidding obstacles, but I know the Lord my God is with me, and He has given me a plan . . . with the victory already won!"

What a mighty battle cry! Here we go, fellow stepmoms, here we go.

TWO

Accept Your Reality—Your Situation, Your Stepkids, Your Husband, and Your Hope

Get ready to cross the Jordan River.

—Joshua 1:2

Carol and Kathi

Six months into the job of full-time stepmother, I (Carol) experienced my most memorable Halloween since trick-or-treating twenty years earlier. I normally enjoyed staying home passing out candy and admiring creative costumes—a computer, a box of Kleenex, a baked potato. I expected this night to be no different. I thought it would be lovely for Jim (and provide consistency for Abby) to continue the tradition of taking his six-year-old daughter trick-or-treating, which both of them enjoyed. I would stay home and continue *my* tradition of keeping warm and taste testing fun-sized Snickers.

This first Halloween, however, Jim thought it could be a good bonding experience if I took Abby on her quest for goodies while he stayed home to pass out treats. I eyed the Snickers. This could also be a good bonding experience for Jim and the chocolate. But I could see he had made a good point.

More than anything, I wanted to build a relationship with my stepdaughter. I wanted to make her life as good as possible. I wanted *my* life to be as good as possible. I wanted our family to love each other. So with a nod to a costume, I donned a black sweatshirt and sweatpants pulled from the back of my closet in an attempt to resemble, ever so faintly, a black cat. I used my eyebrow pencil to fill in a few carefully placed "whiskers," and I was good to go.

Abby and I were excited as we joined other trick-or-treaters on the street. This was fun.

After tromping through the neighborhood for what I deemed an appropriate amount of time and certainly long enough for me to approach a nearly frozen state, we walked expectantly up a neighbor's driveway toward the front door.

Little did I know that a heart-stopping moment awaited around the corner. There, lurking just out of sight from behind a parked car, a hunchbacked Quasimodo lunged out of the dark directly at us, grunting loudly. Even more terrifying, the costumed character continued chasing us back down the driveway and onto the street. Abby and I screamed and ran toward home, hampered by her wind-whipped costume that bound her legs so tight she could barely scoot, much less run. I thought she resembled a geisha, and smiled even in my fear.

We reached home with pounding hearts, gasping for breath. Jim met us in the driveway, after hearing our screams. We reported our adventure to him, and soon the three of us were doubled over in laughter. A golden moment, perhaps even bonding. I thought it seemed like a fun note on which to end the evening. *Could we be done now?* I wondered. I checked my watch. Too early to stop. Did Jim want to switch places with me? No, keep going, he suggested. This was good. With one raised eyebrow, I glanced at the dwindling Snickers supply. There hadn't been that many trick-or-treaters; Jim and the Snickers were bonding.

So off Abby and I went again. We approached the next driveway with stealth, relaxing only after we made it to the door without being attacked. And then it happened. Right before she reached out to ring the doorbell, Abby looked up at me in her Strawberry Shortcake mask, with what I knew was a smile underneath, and something happened in my heart. The same thing happened in hers. A connection. Love. Trust. God's resounding "Yes!" to our all prayers. *This stepmom thing just might work out,* I thought.

Six months of fixing her favorite mac and cheese, six months of playing endless games of Candy Land, six months of scripting stories starring Strawberry Shortcake dolls all paid off in that one unforgettable moment more than thirty years ago.

For us as stepmothers to enjoy the "promised land" of a fulfilling marriage and family life, we enter the lives of our stepchildren roaring like the Jordan River in flood stage—personalities already developed, habits already established, loyalties already entrenched. Wounded through no fault of their own by the breakup of their families through death or divorce, our stepchildren have also spent time wandering in the desert, dragging their baggage with them. Now *they* face a flooding Jordan River to cross—living life in a stepfamily, including incorporating a stepmother into their lives. We want them to accept and love us; they usually just want us to go away.

At first glance, God's order to the children of Israel to cross the Jordan River might not seem daunting, but at the time, the Jordan River roared at flood stage, making it seemingly impassable. Did God realize the difficulty of the task He had given them?

Each stepmother, too, must prepare to plunge into raging waters. The first step is to accept our own set of tough family circumstances as we begin the hard work of stepmothering with grace. We can't address problems effectively until we accept their reality, yet we find it harder than we expected to give up our dreams of how life should be. Taking that first step is a brave act of obedience, with the promise of blessings to follow. But who expected it to be so *hard*?

While there is no end to the variety of individual circumstances we each face, the acceptance of three realities is crucial to the success of every stepmother. We need to accept our situations, our stepchildren, and our husbands.

1. Accept Your Situation

This seems obvious, as truthfully, it is all you have to work with. Getting a handle on this first step will help you avoid the danger of unrealistic expectations, which can set you up for overwhelming disappointments and heartache.

I (Kathi) kept thinking that once my fiancé's kids saw how much I loved them, things would get better. Then Roger and I got married.

Jeremy, my sixteen-year-old future stepson, refused to come to our wedding unless his mom was invited. (You could say we were a little fuzzy on boundaries back then. Yes, my husband's ex-wife was at our wedding.) Jeremy refused to stand up for his dad at the wedding because he felt as if he were betraying his mom. And then he spent the whole ceremony crying. That's when I realized that this whole blended-family thing wasn't going to get magically better because I loved God and I loved Roger and his kids.

My encouragement to you? Start where you are. Whatever your circumstances, face them realistically and accept them fully. They are *your* circumstances; this is your life. Embrace it.

I (Carol) especially want to remind you that even if it's hard to accept that you don't have the biblical ideal of one man, one woman, and the children of that union for life, you're not alone, stepmom. There are so many blended families all over the world today. Indeed, many of our most revered biblical heroes—Abraham, Jacob, David, Ruth, to name a few—didn't experience ideal family situations either. Even Jesus grew up with half brothers and half sisters and was reared by a man who contributed nothing to His DNA! He understands firsthand the challenges of living in a stepfamily. And He will help you meet your challenges with success.

Acceptance is the first key to making what you do have—even if not ideal—excellent. "When we accept the way things are, we stop fighting for what cannot be and become content with what is,"[1] write psychologists Henry Cloud and John Townsend.

For those couples who stick it out and work through the tough issues of marriage with stepchildren, the results are often exceptionally strong and close relationships. The teamwork and partnership required to weather the ups and downs of stepfamily life contribute to a strong love and appreciation for each other, as well as deep satisfaction in accomplishing a difficult task together.

Accepting our circumstances also empowers us and keeps us from viewing ourselves as victims of them. When we bring our challenges to God and invite His participation in them, an inner peace and confidence reminds us that those challenges and circumstances are in good hands. "Every problem is a character-building opportunity, and the more difficult it is, the greater the potential for building spiritual muscle and moral fiber," writes Pastor Rick Warren in *The Purpose-Driven Life*. "If you will give God all your distasteful, unpleasant experiences, he will blend them together for good."[2]

That's the kind of blending we can realistically expect to happen in our stepfamilies. And it's good.

2. ACCEPT YOUR STEPCHILDREN

It can be hard to accept a child's looks, personality, habits, hygiene, manners, behavior, morals, attitudes, style of dress, speech, choice of friends, music, immaturity, life skills, and feelings—all of which you have had no opportunity to influence up to this point. It's easy to think (whether realistically or not), *Have mercy! I would never have allowed that trait to develop if I had reared this child from birth!* (As if we have that much control!) And maybe you wouldn't have, but it's what you've got to work with now.

We want to make our stepchildren over into *our* image of what they should be, especially since they share our names and our homes, even if on a part-time basis. How to cope? Accept the truth that Jesus loves and accepts you just the way you are, and He will help you love and accept your stepchildren just the way they are. Sound easy? It's not.

"I confess, I can't do it by myself," Jennifer confided, "so every day I ask Jesus to help me accept and love my stepchildren . . . even though I don't always like them very much. It keeps me very close to Him, and that makes it all worthwhile." For many stepmoms, accepting their stepchildren means making a commitment to their well-being, no matter what.

In fact, having you in their lives may be the best thing that ever happens to your stepchildren, whether they realize and acknowledge it or not. Several stepmothers told me they were the ones who had the privilege of introducing their stepchildren to Jesus. Others instructed their stepchildren in such basic disciplines as saying please and thank you, brushing their teeth, and even knowing how often to shower.

When we accept our stepchildren, we are treating them the way God wants us to, which honors Him and blesses us as well. Accepting our stepchildren isn't the same thing as condoning their actions, however. But it's the best way to encourage the beginnings of change.

3. ACCEPT YOUR HUSBAND

When Roger and I (Kathi) were engaged, one of the things I loved about him was the way he treated me like a princess. He would take me to nice dinners and buy me little presents. I felt loved and cherished.

But when I saw him spending loads of money on his daughter's clothes, or driving to three different restaurants to get him and his kids *three different meals*, I almost lost my mind. It drove me crazy to see the ways he spoiled his kids, especially his daughter.

I brought this up to him one day. His response? "So it's okay when I spoil you but not when I do it for my daughter." Ugh. He got me.

Yes, the very same things that made me fall in love with Roger were the things that drove me crazy about his parenting. One of the things I wish I had remembered is that Amanda was a teenager—not just a stepdaughter. That spoiled-behavior phase? It's something that most teens go through at one point or another. Amanda is a lovely, generous, and thoughtful young woman now. But at that time, both she and I were going through an adjustment phase—and we both needed to know that Roger loved us.

Your husband, like mine (Carol), is going to need a lot of acceptance, a lot of patience, and a lot of forgiveness. Of course, you will, too, and hopefully, you'll get it. In addition to all the usual issues a flawed human being brings into marriage, your husband carries baggage and scars that make your marriage harder. Again, you do, too, especially if you've been married before. That's just reality. So don't be surprised if you find yourself staring some of the following common realities in the face:

- Part of your husband's paycheck belongs to another woman in the form of alimony and to children who aren't yours, in the form of child support.
- His children came before you in time, and they will often come before you in his actions—maybe even his heart.
- Or perhaps, in your opinion, your husband isn't committed *enough* to his children, and that bothers you.
- He carries guilt for his part in a broken marriage and the disruption of his children's lives.

- He has to unlearn old patterns of relating and learn to live with you—and your children, if you had any before this marriage.

Maybe your husband plays "Disneyland Dad" and tries to make up for his children's sufferings by overindulging them, usually to their detriment. Maybe he abdicates his role and won't discipline his children, or leaves the disciplining to you, usually to your detriment. Maybe he refuses to protect and defend you, allowing his children to speak and act rudely to you, always to the children's *and* your detriment—as well as his. These attitudes need to be acknowledged, forgiven, and dealt with. (We'll discuss how in later chapters.)

We need to accept the fact that our husbands are men, not God. This also sounds obvious (some days more than others), but it's tempting to expect your husband to be and do for you what only Jesus can. As wonderful as he is, your husband cannot be a constant source of wisdom, encouragement, comfort, and companionship. Jesus can. Your husband can tire of listening to all your dreams, goals, insecurities, fears, feelings, stories, and every detail of your everyday life. But only Jesus is capable of always being happy to hear from you.

Sometimes when your husband falls short of your expectations, it's easy to blame him, criticize him, and question why he has let you down, when in reality, there is no way he could have fulfilled all your hopes. Jesus is the only one who doesn't get tired, doesn't get annoyed, and doesn't need "me" time or a guys' night out. It's just reality.

What About the Rewards?

Here is the hope for stepmoms: You *will* receive a reward, though it may come later.

Rewards for stepmothers are often long term and a long time coming. Yet God encourages us to keep the end result in mind: "Let us not become weary in doing good, for at the proper time we will reap a harvest if we do not give up" (Galatians 6:9). And "Whatever you do, work at it with all your heart, as working for the Lord, not for men, since you know that you will receive an inheritance from the Lord as a reward. *It is the Lord Christ you are serving*" (Colossians 3:23–24, emphasis added).

It's a lovely experience when stepchildren express appreciation, and I hope you get to hear it one day. If you're like most stepmothers, however, you probably won't receive thanks or encouragement from your stepchildren or, for that matter, most members of your extended stepfamily for at least the first few years, if ever. If you *do*, just be pleasantly surprised and say thank you!

But even if no one else realizes what stepmothering has cost you and the toll it has taken on you and expresses appreciation, *God* knows. He's the One we serve. He sees. He cares. He gives the best rewards. And He will, you know.

After being in the role of stepmom for ten years, I (Kathi) am now starting to see the rewards. I've been fortunate to have a husband who supports me in my role, but he couldn't force his kids to do the same. From our first year, when I told Roger that I thought I'd made the biggest mistake of my life by marrying him, to now, when I consider Amanda and Jeremy to be two of my favorite people in the world and their mom a friend, it's evident that God has performed a miracle in our family. Even when I felt alone in my stepmothering, I wasn't. God was sustaining me every step of the way.

If you're anything like me (Carol), perhaps you've wondered, *Is it wrong to want to be appreciated?* Not at all. God Himself acknowledges, appreciates, and values every effort you make on His behalf to show love to your stepchildren. Check out this verse: "The King will reply, 'I tell you the truth, whatever you did for one of the least of these brothers of mine, you did for me'" (Matthew 25:40).

Remember, you are in this for the long haul. We don't reap in the same season in which we sow. While you are waiting, keep watching.

"I've given up looking for the big reward," related Brenda. "Life isn't fair; I just accept that. Now I do what I do because it's the right thing to do. And actually, once I gave up expecting a big reward, I began to see little ones come my way."

Go back and review God's formula for success in chapter 1. When we bask in God's love for us, obey His Word, and then leave the results with Him, we're successful. God doesn't tell us what our success will look like reflected in the lives of our stepchildren, or when, *if ever*, we can expect to see the results of our faithfulness in their lives. We have a responsibility to them, but we cannot control what they think or how they behave. The quality of our relationships with our stepchildren doesn't determine whether or not we are successful stepmothers.

When the pressures and demands of stepmotherhood overwhelm us, and we scream at God that we can't do this, He gently reminds us that He is with us and asks, "Is *anything* too hard for me?" (Jeremiah 32:27, emphasis added). And so we snuggle close to Him knowing that He loves us and provides all the resources we need.

As stepmoms we're in for a wild ride, and we can't tackle it alone. The good news is, we don't have to. God never intended any of us to handle life alone. We need Him and we need each other as we enter stepfamily life at flood stage. Now *that's* reality! And we have every confidence you can be successful as we go through this journey together.

THREE

It's Not (All) About the Kids

The LORD your God is with you, he is mighty to save.

He will take great delight in you, he will quiet you

with his love, he will rejoice over you with singing.

—ZEPHANIAH 3:17

Kathi

It was one in the morning, the night before our wedding, and I couldn't sleep. Most brides have trouble sleeping because they're excited about the ceremony the next day and becoming Mrs. _____.

But not me. I couldn't sleep because I knew I had to call off the wedding.

You see, Roger had done what I considered (at the time) to be the holy grail of offenses on our wedding week: He went to his son's hockey practice.

I know, I know, it doesn't sound call-off-the-wedding worthy when you read it, but at the time, it was traumatic. You see, Roger and I had made an agreement when we got engaged. The week of our wedding, there was so much going on that, for my own sanity, I needed both of us off kid duty. School was out for the year, and there was no place our kids *had* to be. I needed a week without extraneous kid commitments so that we could concentrate on our out-of-town guests and the little party with two hundred of our closest friends. Roger's kids were still with him, and my kids were with me, and they were all getting fed on a regular basis, but if one of our four teenagers wanted to go to the mall, they either needed to ask their other parent or walk.

On Friday, after the wedding rehearsal, our whole wedding party, including Roger's family from Georgia, went out to our favorite Italian restaurant to celebrate. At the end of the night, we all stood around in the parking lot saying our good-byes and looking forward to the wedding the next day. As I kissed Roger good night, he casually mentioned that he and his brothers were going to watch his son, Jeremy, practice hockey in the morning.

My heart dropped. Hockey on the morning of our wedding? Um, no.

I held it together while standing there in the parking lot among all our friends and family, but as soon as I got into the car, I burst into tears.

I got back to my hotel room, where I was bunking with my friend Shannon and my daughter, Kimberly. When Kimberly fell asleep in the other room, I had a heart-to-heart with Shannon. I was trying desperately to figure out why I was so emotional over the fact that Roger wanted to go see Jeremy play hockey. After several hours of discussion, I finally came to my conclusion: My biggest fear was that I was going to come in second to Roger's kids for the rest of my life, and I felt like that was playing out before me the night before my wedding. I was heartbroken. I knew that I would be miserable for the rest of my life if that was the case. I'd already been miserable in one marriage, and I wasn't about to do it a second time.

So I called Roger and told him, "I can't marry you."

It was two in the morning, and Roger came right over to the hotel. While Shannon and Kimberly were in the bedroom, Roger and I sat out in the front room of the suite and talked. I told him that I loved him more than anyone in the world, and that if he didn't feel the same way or couldn't live the same way, putting me in the position right after

God and right before his kids, this marriage wasn't going to work, and I needed to get out before I made another mistake.

He assured me that I was his top priority after God. Good man, right? Then we proceeded to have a long, hard conversation. But it was a conversation that we needed to have.

It feels selfish to have these conversations, to ask our spouses to put us before their own children. I know that I felt split down the middle. I didn't want to be the demanding new wife; I also wanted Roger to maintain a strong relationship with his kids.

We've all seen and heard the horror stories about dads ignoring their kids after wife number two comes on the scene. None of us is looking for that. And if you're reading a book about how to be the most effective stepmom you can be, I can guarantee you aren't one of those second wives who doesn't care about your stepkids. You care deeply about your stepkids, but let's admit it: This is hard stuff. You are trying to balance the needs you have as a wife with the best interests of some very needy (and possibly broken) kids, and this situation can breed discontent and jealousy and make you act in ways you never thought you would.

You want to be the perfect loving and giving stepmom, but there are times you may also want to throw a hissy fit and scream, "Hey! I'm your *wife*! What about me?!"

The smart and brave couple wisely says, "It's not all about the kids."

Author Ron Deal says, "Your children will never suffer neglect because you make a strong commitment to your new spouse. You don't have to choose between your spouse and your children; when you make your marriage your primary priority, you are actually choosing both. Placing your spouse in the 'front seat' of your heart is good for your children, too. In fact, a healthy marriage means safety and protection for children."[1]

This can feel counterintuitive. You want your kids to know they are loved and adored. It's natural. But more than anything, kids in a blended family need to know they are safe. They need to know the rules, to know where they stand. They need to know that the leaders of the home are on the same page. And that they are expected to make their own way at some point, because you and their dad are in the marriage thing for the long haul and will be in love long after they've left the house. That's a healthy way for your stepkids to grow up.

Here are some basic rules Roger and I created to make sure that our kids saw us as a united front:

- *Decisions are made away from the kids.* Whenever a child wanted something from us, if it was a big enough decision, Roger and I always said the same thing, "Let me talk it over with _____ and get back to you." This did a few things for us: (1) It gave us the time and space to think and pray about our decision; (2) it kept us from being upset that something was decided without consulting the other person; and (3) it didn't let us get swayed by cute eyes and pouty lips.

- *Decisions are presented as a team.* That meant that I, as the stepmom, never had to take on additional bad-guy roles. Roger and I discussed the decision as a team and came to a decision as a team. Plus, it gave Roger the opportunity to say things like, "My first instinct was to say no, but Kathi pointed out that you've been doing your chores without being asked, and she believes you can handle the extra responsibility." (Anytime a dad can put the stepmom in the position of being on the stepchild's "side," it's a good thing.)

- *Kids are reminded that they are always loved.* Just as in a non-blended family, the first relationship after the one with God is the relationship of husband and wife. I get it. After what the kids have been through (dealing with questions like *Who is this new woman, and why is she trying to take away our dad?*), this isn't an easy task. So while you and your spouse are establishing your relationship, it's important that he keep his relationship with his kids a top priority as well. A lot of work? You bet.

Along with presenting a united front before the kids, balancing relationships is vital. Roger was very intentional about making sure we had a date night every week, but he also made sure that he spent time with each of his kids. I know it's easy to feel jealous of the time our husbands spend with their kids, but instead of ever making them feel guilty about it, we need to encourage and celebrate the fact that they take being a dad seriously, and it will pay off later.

When I asked my stepkids what were some of the things I did right, by the grace of God (because I made plenty of mistakes), one thing they both said was that I encouraged them and their dad to spend time together.

Some friends of ours have had the hardest time navigating these relationship waters. Our friend Dan remarried when his daughter was seventeen, and it has been traumatic for everyone involved. Dan's daughter is upset because she's had her dad to herself for so long, and now there is a new woman. Dan's new wife is devastated because she feels like she's in second place in this new family, and Dan is torn all the time between his new wife and his daughter.

Our advice in situations like this? Get to a counselor. Now!

When you have such huge dynamics in a family, really your best option is to make everyone seek counseling. Everyone. These are rough waters you all are facing, and it's critical that the situation be handled with strong boundaries, buckets of compassion, and tons of love for all the hurting parties.

So if our focus isn't on the kids, then where does it lie?

It's About Your Relationship with God

Being a stepmom is not only a humbling role, but it's downright hard. So often, that role involves all the responsibilities of a mom without the relationship of a mom with the kids. Many times as a stepmom, you are responsible for a lot of the day-to-day activities that your stepkid is involved in—seeing that homework is done, showers are taken, and uniforms are washed, to name just a few.

And yet your stepchildren probably aren't standing up and cheering you on in your role, referring to you as a modern-day Proverbs 31 woman, or rising up and calling you blessed. Add to that a husband who is stressed both emotionally and financially, and then throw in your stepkids' mom, who may or may not be your biggest fan (okay, probably not), and it could lead even the most grounded woman to have a serious inferiority complex.

Even the best of kids can smell weakness and use it to their advantage. That's one of the major reasons stepmoms need to stay strong. And the only way I've found to stay truly strong is to see myself through God's eyes, not through the eyes of my stepkids, my husband's ex-wife, or even the people "on my side" (like my husband, my own kids, my family). The only way we can walk with strength through this stepmothering journey is to walk in the light of God's view of us: That we are smart, equipped, cherished, and protected. We are God's. If we start to accept the way others view us as our reality, we're going to always feel like we are not enough. When I'm starting to see myself only through the eyes of those around me, it's a great time to be reminded of how God sees me. Here are some of my go-to verses:

We are God's workmanship, created in Christ Jesus to do good works, which God prepared in advance for us to do. (Ephesians 2:10)

In all ... things we are more than conquerors through him who loved us. (Romans 8:37)

You did not choose me, but I chose you and appointed you to go and bear fruit—fruit that will last. Then the Father will give you whatever you ask in my name. (John 15:16)

> The LORD delights in those who fear him,
>> who put their hope in his unfailing love.
>>> (Psalm 147:11)

> You are forgiving and good, O LORD,
>> abounding in love to all who call to you.
>>> (Psalm 86:5)

You are a chosen people, a royal priesthood, a holy nation, a people belonging to God, that you may declare the praises of him who called you out of darkness into his wonderful light. (1 Peter 2:9)

Who shall separate us from the love of Christ? Shall trouble or hardship or persecution or famine or nakedness or danger or sword? As it is written: "For your sake we face death all day long; we are considered as sheep to be slaughtered." No, in all these things we are more than conquerors through him who loved us. For I am convinced that neither death nor life, neither angels nor demons, neither the present nor

the future, nor any powers, neither height nor depth, nor
anything else in all creation, will be able to separate us from
the love of God that is in Christ Jesus our Lord. (Romans
8:35–39)

I can do everything through him who gives me strength.
(Philippians 4:13)

You are a people holy to the LORD your God. The LORD your
God has chosen you out of all the peoples on the face of the earth
to be his people, his treasured possession. (Deuteronomy 7:6)

To stay strong as a stepmom, you need to get into God's Word and
stay there. His view of you is the only one that matters. Don't let others
determine your worth as a person or determine your worth by the kind
of job you're doing as a stepmom. Only God gets to determine your
worth on days when you're feeling like Carol Brady from *The Brady
Bunch*, and on other days when you're feeling like a wicked stepmother
in a Disney film.

IT'S ABOUT YOUR RELATIONSHIP
WITH YOUR HUSBAND

When Roger and I first got married, he made one of the most unselfish
sacrifices ever: He gave me permission not to find a job right away so
that I could pursue a career in writing and speaking.

That's when I had to let him know that he was crazy.

"You're taking on me and my two kids with no additional support.
And if I'm speaking and writing, not only will I not be making money,

but it will probably *cost* us money for me to go to conferences and take classes. No. I need to get a job."

But he was insistent. "Kathi, I believe in you, and I believe that God has a calling on your life. It's one of the reasons I fell in love with you, and I want to support you in it. We'll cut costs, we'll budget, we'll make it happen."

And so with fear and trepidation, Roger and I blended our two families, his adult-sized bank account with my tiny one, and all our worldly possessions. Roger kept working, and while I stayed home managing the comings and goings of our new brood, I also took tiny steps toward launching my own speaking and writing career.

We'd already decided that all of our kids would be attending the public schools closest to our home. The schools weren't fancy, but they had good ratings and were within walking distance of our house. With Roger working in another city and all three of our school-age kids living with us (Roger's older daughter was no longer in school), it was doable to only have to go to one junior high and one high school each day. However, this decision didn't sit well with Roger's ex-wife. Roger had been sending his son to a very expensive private school that, while very prestigious, didn't seem to be helping Jeremy academically, socially, athletically, or emotionally. But Jeremy's mom was determined that he should stay in that school.

When Roger explained to her that we couldn't send one child to a private school and the other two to public schools, that he had seen no advantage to Jeremy being in that school, and that we needed to do what was best for the entire family, she came back at him with, "Well, tell Kathi to go get a job; then you could afford for Jeremy to go to private school." I get it. She wanted the best for her child. But as a blended family, we had to consider what was best for all our kids.

Roger is a pretty nonconfrontational kind of guy, but he took no time setting her straight. "That is none of your business. Kathi and I have talked and prayed about this, and it's our decision."

Those kinds of conversations can tear at the fiber of a remarriage. The needs and wants of the kids, the desires of the ex-wife, and the pressures of making it all work can strain a family. That's why it's so important to make sure that right after your relationship with God, the next most important relationship in your home is between you and your husband.

Since Roger and I had talked through these decisions and prayed about them, we were better equipped to stand up and be bold with the plans we'd made for our marriage that also affected the rest of our family. Nope, we didn't get it perfect. Ever. But we came to a place where we could speak to each of our exes with respect, and we set boundaries, knowing that our kids were and are our top priorities after God and our marriage.

While it's important to keep your relationship with your husband a priority, it's also vital that in all the serious business of blending a family, you and your husband have some serious fun along the way. Remember, the reason this whole blended-family thing is happening is because you and your husband fell in love against all common sense (and maybe a couple of kids' wishes). This marriage thing can truly be fun!

Make sure there's plenty of intentional dating, flirting, touching, and loving in your marriage. Blended family or not, our kids need to see that healthy, happy couples hold hands, smile, and brag on each other; love to work on projects together; cook together; and occasionally lock the bedroom door and don't come out.

Our daughter Amanda has been dating a young man, Shaun, for a few years. One night we were sitting around our backyard fire pit playing the You Rock game for my husband's birthday. In this game, everyone goes around a circle and tells the birthday boy or girl why they rock. When it came to Shaun, he said, "Roger, someday I'm going to make Amanda my wife, and I know the kind of husband I want to be to her, because I've seen the kind of husband you've been to Kathi."

After I sobbed uncontrollably (because that's what I do), Roger and I stayed up late talking about what Shaun had said. Yes, the fact that Roger is a connected, loving husband has benefited me in ways I could never even describe. But now it's benefiting his daughter, my stepdaughter, Amanda, because of the example he's set.

So go make out with your man. It will benefit generations to come!

It's About You

It's easy to get lost in the world of being a stepmom. By listening to all the advice that well-meaning (if not well-informed) people want to give you, you could spend sixteen hours every day serving your husband, your stepkids, and your kids in an effort to do everything right. But that's a surefire way of burning out.

The demands of being a stepmom can be all-consuming. That's why it's so important to disengage from the intensity and find ways to de-stress and nurture ourselves. Here are a few suggestions:

1. *Engage in activities that make you feel like a winner.* Some stepmoms rockclimb; some run marathons. I cook. I knew when I got married that I was a pretty decent cook. Not gourmet by any stretch of the imagination, but I could throw together a respectable marinara and make a batch of million-dollar chocolate-chip cookies without a recipe. And as I tried new recipes (like pad thai, couscous, and eggplant parmesan), I felt my confidence building every day. I wasn't feeling like a million dollars as a stepmom, but when I cooked and baked it made me feel like even if I wasn't winning in every area of my life, there were still things I could do.

One of my friends started a kickboxing class the year she became a stepmom. Another friend told me that she started painting classes just to get out of the house, but then she realized that they weren't only getting her away from family drama; they were giving her something to feel proud of and achieve weekly.

Most of the stepmoms I know work outside the home in addition to all their responsibilities at home. While I respect each family's choice in this area, I was so glad to have a job (even if it was working from home) that affirmed me on a regular basis. Yes, our identity needs to be firmly established in Christ. But it's also great to do things with both long-term payoffs (stepparenting) and short-term rewards (the satisfaction of a job well done at work).

2. *Hang out with people who don't resent you for marrying their father.* It's easy to be all about the family, especially when you're in this high-pressure cooker of a family. One of the best things Roger did for me was to encourage me to hang out with friends. I'd meet them for coffee, or lunch, and we'd talk about real grown-up things instead of the constant back-and-forth of all the family stuff. I was a nicer person when I got home, and my husband considered it a smart investment.

3. *Make sure you have some off-duty hours.* It's incredibly hard to go off duty when you have little ones, but the constant stress of being in a blended family can take its toll on you not just emotionally but physically as well. I'm in a better place emotionally, spiritually, physically, and mentally when I've taken some time to invest in myself. Having a morning devotional time, going on a walk with my dog, going to the gym and working out on the treadmill and stationary bike, and even just having time to sit on the back patio and read a book that nourishes my soul are all ways that make me a better person.

It's difficult when you feel as though you have to keep trying harder to make this whole stepmom thing work, but for most of us, it's not about trying harder. It's about *trusting* harder. Trusting that God has given you enough hours and enough days to do everything that needs to get done. Trusting that God brought you and your husband together for a reason. Trusting that your strengths and weaknesses complement your husband's. Trusting that God didn't make a mistake.

4. *Hang out with your own kids . . . alone.* If you brought your own kids into the marriage, make sure that you're spending time with them one-on-one as well. Not everything has to be a group activity. This is especially important as your kids get older.

When Roger and I blended our families, all of our kids were teens. My kids and I already had solid relationships built on thirteen and fourteen years of being together. I couldn't just jump ahead in my relationships with my stepkids, and I didn't want to step back in my relationships with my own kids. So while we did a lot of things together as a blended family, Roger and I also did things just with our own kids.

Justen, Kimberly, and I listened to a lot of books on CD or downloaded to my iPod when just the three of us were driving in the car. One of our favorite books, *The Prize Winner of Defiance, Ohio*, was being made into a small, independent movie. My husband and his kids had absolutely no desire to see this film, so Justen, Kimberly, and I loaded up on candy, got our giant tub of popcorn, and watched the movie together in pure delight. After the show we went out to dinner and talked about the movie and life for my junior high and high school kids.

Along the way, our family has done several of these "Hunter kids only" dates (Hunter is my kids' last name). We've also done "Lipp kids only" dates, and even some girls-only and boys-only dates. Splitting off into these smaller groups has definitely worked for our large family. Initially when we were blending, there was an ease that came with only hanging out with my kids every once in a while. Now that our family has really blended, any combination of the kids is easy, but it did take a very long time to get there.

I've heard of other families that take the no-man-left-behind strategy to blended families—if one person goes, everyone goes. But in our family, it seemed silly to deny the very real past that Roger and I each had with our own kids. We still continue to do things as a big family (celebrations, vacations, Sunday-night dinners), but we also continue to do things one-on-one with our kids, and sometimes with the family of origin.

It's Also About the Kids
(Just Not *All* About Them)

I know that one of the deepest longings of my heart, and yours as well, I imagine, is to have loving relationships with your stepkids. So yes, it is about them. But in the stepparenting game, your relationships with your stepkids are like no other relationships you have in your life. You can "work" on other relationships, but with stepkids, how they see you in the light of your relationships with other people—God, their dad, their mom, your own kids, and so on—really matters. And nothing will test who you really are and whose you are more than being a stepmom.

While I was a single mom, I worked in an office that had its share of challenges. The boss was disrespectful, some of the coworkers were challenging, and I couldn't wait to get home and not deal with those people for another fourteen hours. For many years, I was living a double life, acting one way in public when faced with problems and then falling apart when I got home.

But what happens when the people you are struggling with live under your roof? There's no place to run. There's no place to hide.

With my stepkids, if I wanted to experience peace, I had to find it even in the midst of some not-so-peaceful situations. Was this faith I talked about real or something I just pulled out when I was in public? Could I truly love my neighbor when that neighbor was fifteen and resented me for moving into his house and moving in on his dad?

The answer, it turns out, was yes.

It was hard, and oh how we struggled, but one of the greatest gifts that being a stepmom has given me is putting my trust in God in real and tangible ways.

I now have experienced mercy, where before I felt judgment.

I now know peace, when before I felt only strife.

I can now love those who are unlovely.

I can now ask for forgiveness when I've messed up. Again and again.

When you're a stepmom, the luxury of a public you and a real you ceases to exist. Your stepkids are going to see how you treat their dad when you disagree. They are going to see how you talk about their mom. They are going to know if you're trying to love them with your whole heart or are just waiting for the moment when you and their dad can live on your own.

No, I don't have control over how my stepkids see me, but I do have control over what I show my stepkids. I want to show them a woman who loves God, loves their dad, and loves them to the best of my ability.

Trying harder probably won't get you very far. But being patient, trusting God, loving your husband beyond reason, and being consistent in all your kids' lives will give you a strong foundation as you build a relationship with your stepkids for the future.

FOUR

Setting Up Systems

Everything should be done in a fitting and orderly way.

—1 Corinthians 14:40

Kathi

Can we just admit that while this stepparenting thing can be rewarding, it brings a complexity to our lives that wasn't there before?

I am not an organized and orderly person by nature. I was never one to color-code my socks or, like my friend Robin in high school, write down everything I wore every day on a calendar so I wouldn't wear the same outfit again for three weeks. Nope, I was more of a "Hey, this looks clean. And it smells clean! Score!" high schooler.

Though my laundry habits improved over time, my natural tendency toward order didn't really improve. But, hey, I was able to keep my kids alive and food on the table just by working hard! It was all fine.

And then I had stepkids.

Suddenly every weakness (and there were a lot of them) that I'd ever had came out in full force. I needed help and fast.

When asked, I offer all blended-family newbies two pieces of practical advice:

1. Get some counseling—even if you think you won't need it.
2. Ask every blended family you know for their best piece of advice.

GETTING ADVICE FROM A COUNSELOR

We've touched on this briefly in the previous chapter, but the reason I give everyone the first piece of advice is because most people only go to see a therapist when they are either at the end of their rope or failing on all fronts. But let's be clear: As a blended family, you are in a difficult situation already, and you need all the help you can get, not because you're failing, but because this stuff is really, really hard.

Even though Roger and I saw a counselor when we planned to get married, we waited to go back until things blew up in our faces after we married. But we did end up back there. And there we were, sitting on the couch in the therapist's office again, trying to work through our issues. And the part that felt unfair was that they weren't our issues; they were my stepson Jeremy's.

Not long after Roger and I got married, the long, slow simmer that had been Jeremy's moodiness boiled over into outright hostility, mostly directed at me. So Roger and I did what parents and stepparents all over the country do. We called a local Christian counselor and requested an appointment for him to see (and fix) Jeremy (at least that's what I was hoping in my heart of hearts).

But instead of scheduling an appointment for Jeremy, the counselor set up a time for Roger and me to come in. The therapist wanted to make sure that we were doing all we could to support Jeremy and help him through this difficult transition.

I have to admit, at first this made me crazy. Of course I was doing everything I could for Jeremy. I was being nice (even though I never felt as though I received any kindness back). I drove him to all his practices and to school. I made really delicious meals at least five times a week and did everything I knew to do to support him.

Clearly Jeremy was the one who needed fixing, not me!

But as Roger and I trudged to those appointments once a week, I started to develop an understanding of my role as a stepmom. At this point, I represented the death of Jeremy's dream of having a whole family again. To him, I was the reason his parents would never get back together again. It gave me sympathy and understanding to understand why I was the enemy. It also gave Roger tools to help support me during this difficult transition—because in hindsight, I needed a lot of support too.

This was the beginning of Roger and Jeremy's long walks at night, where they could sort out Jeremy's feelings and angst without my having to hear about it. This was also the beginning for Roger in learning how to support his son. And this was the beginning for me in letting go of my must-be-the-perfect-stepmom expectations and learning to just be me.

None of this would have ever happened without the support of our therapist. We went to him because while we each had two kids, neither of us were parenting experts, and we needed an expert in our corner as we worked through all of these issues.

I was trying so hard not to come off as the wicked stepmom. I figured if I was nice to my stepkids, we could avoid all the blended-family drama. But in my mind, "nice" meant giving in. And giving in just to keep the peace is a sure way to set up your stepfamily for failure. What we needed to do was learn to love and respect each other while keeping boundaries intact. With some therapy, I learned the following:

- *To keep my expectations realistic.* I fell into the same trap so many engaged couples fall into. "As long as we're a loving home, everything will work out!" Love is important, but for the most part, my role in my stepkids' lives was to provide stability. They didn't want hugs and kisses; they wanted to know when dinner was going to be ready, who was picking them up, and if they had clean clothes. The love part came much later.

- *To focus on the issue at hand.* Our issue was blending our family. But it would have been so easy to bring other issues into the mix (in-laws, finances, who needed to pick up dinner, etc.). When Roger and I were in counseling, we could stay on the same side of the issue and be *for* each other, not against each other.
- *To figure out systems for our house to reduce stress for everyone.* Honestly, sometimes a quick checklist or set of rules is what it takes to figure out exactly what to do to work through a tough time. And our counselor helped us do just that.

GETTING ADVICE FROM OTHER
BLENDED FAMILIES

While our therapist helped us deal with a lot of the emotional fallout in our blended family, a lot of practical issues needed to be addressed as well. I feel that one of the reasons our blended family survived (and sometimes, occasionally, even thrived) was because we received some key advice from other blended families:

1. *Talk early, talk often.* As mentioned, even before Roger and I got married, we started seeing a family counselor to talk through the inevitable issues that would come up. We knew we'd need a third party who wasn't on Roger's side, my side, or any of the kids' sides, but was on our family's side.

2. *Take notes.* Oh, it feels awful to have to get everything in writing, but I've come to understand that sometimes you need to refer back to what your husband, your stepkids, or their mom said. I finally got to the point where I would either (a) hold a conversation by e-mail if I had a discussion with any other parent, or (b) sum up the conversa-

tion in an e-mail and send it to the person I was speaking with.

So if Roger asked me to pick up his kids at school on Tuesday and Thursday at three thirty, I would just send him an e-mail clarifying the time and place. It kept us from having hurt feelings from a misunderstanding later on. (This is especially helpful when other family members seem to "forget" conversations that you've had. Always go back to the e-mail!)

3. *Keep a household calendar.* If you're sharing custody of your stepkids with another person or family, having a household calendar is a *must* so that you can keep track of everyone's comings and goings (and so that there are no surprises). Kids need to know when they will be hanging out where, who will be picking up whom, and so on. Having a huge calendar was a must in our home (ours was eighteen inches tall and twenty-four inches wide, with giant boxes to write on). I kept it in the kitchen so everyone could clearly keep tabs on the schedule.

4. *Send group texts.* When schedules are complicated for older kids, I like to include in a group text everyone who needs to be informed. That way we all know what's happening and what the expectations are.

5. *Set house rules.* Yep, the rules may be different at your stepkids' other parent's home. For our family, unless there are special circumstances, we have rules, and while our kids are living at this house, these are the rules.

6. *Have a Facebook page.* Since our kids are all at the age where they're using Facebook, when we have a family event or something they all need to know about, we just create an event on Facebook to give everyone the details.

OTHER "STEPSTUFF" TO DISCUSS
WITH YOUR SPOUSE

Celebrations

In engineering, there's an old saying: "You can have it better, cheaper, or faster. Pick two out of three." It's true. How can you have a better-quality product made cheaper and delivered ahead of schedule? It might be possible, but you'll kill the engineer in the process.

Roger and I have adopted a similar motto for family celebrations: "You can celebrate on the right day, you can have the whole family together, or you can have people be happy about it. Pick two out of three."

With blended families, holidays put stress not only on you and your husband but on your stepkids as well. They may feel responsible for keeping loyalties and keeping the peace. You probably feel responsible for keeping things from blowing up!

Roger and I realized early on in our marriage that two things were important when it came to holidays: having everyone together, and having everyone happy (or as happy as possible) about it. The date? That really didn't matter to either of us. But it did matter to my stepkids' mom and to my ex-husband, so we took a different route: We celebrated on an entirely different day. For our family, Christmas was on December 13 or 22, when we could all go to a cabin at Lake Tahoe to celebrate together. Some years, Thanksgiving turned into food and fun the Friday after.

Another important note about the holidays: Our first year trying the "celebrate on a different day" tactic worked out great—almost. We celebrated Christmas on December 23, and then Roger and I took a trip to a few different bed-and-breakfasts around Northern California, even staying in a tree-house apartment over Christmas Eve and Christmas. It seemed like the perfect arrangement: Celebrate with the kids and then have a couple's celebration of our own. (We even brought our own portable Christmas tree on our little trip.)

What we didn't find out until we called the kids on Christmas Day was that some of them were sitting at our house with nowhere to go. Yes, they needed to be at their other parent's house on Christmas, but that celebration lasted about three hours, and then the kids were done. Now, even though we usually celebrate on a day other than the holiday, Roger and I are always around on the actual day so that our kids can drop by. Eventually everyone stops over, and we end up eating lots of leftovers and playing loud games of hand-and-foot canasta or Bang around the kitchen table.

Another issue we had with the holidays was who we were celebrating with. Roger and his ex-wife had fallen into the habit of celebrating holidays together. (Roger looks back on that practice as not one of his better choices. His personality lends itself to keeping the peace, and that's what he was trying to do.) This may work for some families, but our counselor told us it can also make it harder on the kids to accept a new spouse into the family. For us, it was time to stop the combined Christmases.

That was a painful transition for Roger's whole family, but in the end it gave us the freedom to celebrate the way we wanted to without the other parent's expectations being put on us. We still celebrated some birthdays and graduations together when it made sense, but we first needed to establish our own home and traditions.

Now that we've been married for almost ten years, and Roger's ex isn't part of our day-to-day lives, we've found it easier to be more open and include her in some of our celebrations. When her kids asked last year if she could come to one of our holiday celebrations, my immediate reaction was "Um . . . really?" (Again, mercy is something I'm working on.) But the more I thought and prayed about it, the more I realized that we were in a different place. Roger's kids weren't asking because they wanted to shut me out. They were asking because they enjoyed our celebrations and wanted to include their mom. So we extended the invite.

She didn't end up coming to the celebration, but it didn't matter. It signaled a change in our family. We were past all the day-to-day drama and could include people who were important to our kids. Now we celebrate almost every birthday with their mom, and it works out great. We have the party at our house, she brings her kids' favorite cakes and even does the dishes!

For my stepdaughter's most recent birthday, I asked if her mom was bringing her new boyfriend. Amanda responded, "I'm not sure. He's afraid it will be awkward. But I told him that you and my dad were the least awkward people around and that he should definitely come." He did come and we had a great time.

This may never work for your family—and maybe it never should. That's okay. Or maybe you do celebrate with your ex or your husband's ex-wife. That's okay, too. Just make sure you have clear communication with your husband about how all of this is making each of you feel and whether it's the best thing for your whole family. It's a beautiful thing when all of your kids' divorced parents can get together in the same room, and your kids don't have to fear the awkwardness. And you can be a huge part in making that happen.

Each year Roger and I needed to ask ourselves, "What honors the kids? What honors our marriage?" I understand that my husband's ex was a big part of his life for a long time. Roger is still friends with some of her family, and I'm fine with that. We've reached a point where we are both friendly with his ex-wife. It's taken a long time to get here, and I've made a lot of mistakes along the way. The journey hasn't been easy, but our marriage is better for it, and so are our kids.

Birthdays

From day one, Roger and I started celebrating everyone's birthdays in roughly the same way: big dinner at our house on or around the birthday person's special day. The birthday boy or girl gets the choice of food and guests (often it will be friends, and sometimes the other parent), and the five of us (Roger, me, and the other three siblings) will work hard to pull off a celebration that the birthday boy or girl will enjoy.

My advice to you is to have a conversation with your spouse about how birthdays should look for your family. I came from a DIY party background (parties at home), while Roger was more of an on-the-town kind of guy. We made compromises, and now all of our kids know what kind of celebration to look forward to!

Scheduling

My first encouragement: I promise that you will not have to spend the rest of your life sharing a schedule with someone else. Your kids will grow up. I promise. (I know. It doesn't feel like it will ever, ever happen.)

For so many stepfamilies, the courts have decided when the kids will be where. But even with a set schedule, there are the back-and-forth visits and the special occasions to consider. One friend has a Gmail calendar set up for her family that both she and her husband have access to, in addition to another online calendar that is shared with her husband's ex-wife.

However you do your scheduling, Roger and I found that a couple of things were important to keep in mind:

1. *Meet once a week to go over the schedule.* Every day was too much, and once a month was not nearly enough for us. But once a week, we had a working lunch where we brought out our calendars and talked about expectations. It really did

help to make sure we were on the same page figuratively and literally.

2. *Check in each night about the next day.* As we cleaned up the evening dishes after dinner, Roger and I would talk about what the next day looked like. Who needed to be where? What were we going to have for dinner the next night? It was simple stuff, but if we could put a couple of things into motion the night before (defrosting meat for dinner, figuring out if we needed to coordinate a schedule with one of our exes, etc.), it made for a much easier tomorrow.

Dealing with the Emotions of Sharing

Every time I talk to a woman in a blended family, there seems to be something of a slow boil to a full-on boil over going on. It's hard enough dealing with kids and family and drama, but add an ex (or two) to other people's schedules, preferences, and needs, and you've just complicated the whole family dynamic.

I know that I can get emotional about the "sharing" aspect of the holidays and special occasions. Some of my friends have had a hard time with sharing. Especially when their stepkids' mom is criticizing them, or making them feel less than part of the family. I know of one family where the biological mom would spend the entire party saying things like, "When you come to my house for the 'real' party . . ." Here are a few things to realize in this kind of situation:

- Only people who are hurting would say, "When we have the *real* celebration . . ." at a party being held for their child.
- It must be incredibly hard to see another woman throwing a party for your child.

- This really has nothing to do with you or me. Really. It
  wouldn't matter who was in our position; this would be a
  hurtful place for any mom to be in. As stepmoms, we need
  to recognize that and have compassion for the ex-wife.
  When we view it through that lens, instead of feeling bitter,
  we can feel compassion.

The plain truth is that we can plan and we can set up systems, we
can have realistic expectations, and we can try our best to share well,
but nothing will completely take away the awkwardness of blended
situations.

One of the best things you can do is to remember that everyone
coming to the table is limping there. In our brokenness, we're all trying
to make the best of a situation we never would have chosen—and even
grow from it. Never assume that family members are always function-
ing at their most healthy level on such occasions, but do assume that
everyone is trying, to the best of their knowledge and abilities, to do
the best they can with what they have.

FIVE

Stepstuff

Do not love the world or anything in the world.

—1 JOHN 2:15

Kathi and Carol

I (Kathi) brought an unusual cat named Zorro into our marriage under slight (okay, much) protest from Roger. He was and always had been a dog person and had no interest in having a cat. But while I was living at my parents' house when I was single, I got the feeling that my mom was a little sad to be losing me and my two kids but was silently rejoicing to see Zorro hit the road. Zorro and her cat didn't get along at all, so when Roger suggested leaving the cat at my mom's, she was clear: "You take the girl, you take the cat."

I'm so glad he decided to take the package deal!

Interestingly, once we got married, I thought that of all the blending that had gone on in our marriage, Zorro had blended best of all. The cat loved Roger. Adored him. He'd wait by the front door until the master of the house came home. Zorro and Roger found their groove almost instantly.

Zorro and Jeremy? Not so much.

Zorro is the mayor of our little part of the neighborhood, and will meet people at their cars and walk them to their front doors. He even goes on walks with me and my husband and our dog. (I think Zorro just wants to flaunt it in our puggle Jake's face that the dog has to be on a leash, but Zorro the cat doesn't.)

One day I overheard Jeremy and a bunch of his friends coming up the walkway to our house. One of Jeremy's buddies said, "Whoa, dude, that's so weird. That cat is walking with us!" And then Jeremy turned around and said, "Oh yeah, that's just my stepcat."

I remember at the time first being amused and then a little hurt. We'd worked so hard to blend this family, and Jeremy was still calling Zorro his stepcat?

Can we all say it together? This stepstuff is *hard*!

Just being a regular family is hard, but then throw in an extra parent figure, kids who feel torn between two families, and extra schedules to manage, and all this stuff could drive you under the kitchen table, hunkered down with a box of Godiva chocolates in one hand and a Starbucks cup in the other.

So it's best to state these issues right up front, since there is one certainty in all blended families: You're going to run into problems. And because ignoring problems doesn't make them go away. (I'm sure I don't have to say that again.)

Some of the issues Roger and I have had to discuss were . . . well, let's just say they were awkward in some cases and downright uncomfortable in others. I think most stepfamilies face similar issues, so let's talk about them and how to deal with them head-on.

VACATIONS

This may seem like a silly topic. After all, how could stepfamilies *not* enjoy a vacation together? But I've come to find out that having a great vacation is 70 percent about the expectations you go in with.

When Roger and I were engaged, we took all the kids to Disneyland. We talked about the trip for weeks and were looking forward to it. But when Roger reserved a room for his family, and one for mine, I was shocked to find out that he'd booked us at the Grand Californian—the most expensive hotel in the area.

Roger wasn't someone who threw his money around. So when I asked him about it, he was honest with his reasons: "I work very hard, and this is something my kids and I love to do. We only have a short time to be together, and we love staying at the Grand Californian. It feels like a treat, and I wanted you and your kids to feel special too." How could I argue with that?

But our kids had differing expectations as well. Roger's kids' expectations included "Sleep late and stay at the park until it closes." Plus, their family had all sorts of must-do rules. We had to eat at Pizza Port for lunch on the first day so that we could get a FASTPASS later in the day for Space Mountain. We also had to get a certain kind of candy at the Winnie the Pooh store. The list went on and on. My kids just wanted to wander around and enjoy the park. Everyone was slightly grumpy for the first part of the trip because of conflicting expectations.

Now when we go on vacation, expectations are talked about in advance, first between Roger and me and then with the kids. Once we are all clear on expectations, compromises are made in advance as well, not in the heat of the moment. As a result, everyone's vacation goes smoother.

We still eat at Pizza Port, and my kids have taken on the "Disney till you drop!" attitude that Roger and his kids have. Compromise—it's a hard but beautiful thing.

DISCIPLINE

I thought I was a laid-back disciplinarian . . . and then I married Roger. Both of our personalities lean toward the nonconflict side of the spectrum. So not only did we need to have a discipline discussion; we also needed to talk about how to support each other when one of us was disciplining our kids.

There weren't little kids in the house when Roger and I married, so the discipline we had to deal with was all teen stuff. (As a fellow stepmom, you won't be surprised to learn that it was a lot about disrespect.) Very few disciplinary issues needed to be handled in the moment, so it was perfectly okay for me to let Roger discipline his own kids.

For a better perspective on discipline with little kids in a blended family, I asked Carol how she and her husband, Jim, handled it. She shares this story with us:

"I had to spank Abby," I (Carol) sobbed into the phone.

I called Jim at work to tell him the story. He assured me I had done the right thing, but giving Abby that first spanking was one of the hardest and scariest things I had ever done. I was a wreck afterward.

Jim and I had known that discipline of five-year-old Abby could be a make-it-or-break-it part of our marriage. We discussed how she had been disciplined in the past by both biological parents (which included spankings), compared ideas, and agreed on a plan acceptable to both of us.

Parents in each stepfamily need to reach their own conclusions about discipline methods, however. If you haven't already had a serious talk with your spouse about this issue, now is the time. Spanking your stepchild may not be your choice or may not be appropriate in your situation. (Under any circumstances, it should be reserved for a child's younger years and should always be administered with self-control, grace, and love.) The most important thing is to set boundaries and be consistent in enforcing them.

Since Jim's first wife had died, we knew I needed to give Abby plenty of time to accept me. After we married, I couldn't just move in and assume authority. So Jim told Abby, in my presence, that he expected her to treat me and speak to me with respect and to obey me as she would him. We laid out clear expectations for her behavior and predictable consequences for breaking the rules. Jim told her I had his authority to discipline her in his absence, and she understood. We even made a chart titled "Abby Learns Respect and Responsibility," complete with reward stickers, for ready reference. She was excited to earn stickers as positive reinforcement for her good choices.

At first, when we were all together, Jim doled out the discipline, allowing me to ease into life with a kindergartner, learn Jim's and Abby's ways, be the mom, and earn the right to speak into her life. Then came the inevitable. About three months into blended-family life, Abby defied my authority for the first time while just the two of us were home. I knew I had to be brave and follow through on our plan. I hadn't expected it to be so hard. I was afraid she would resent me. I was afraid she wouldn't like me. But this wasn't childish irresponsibility warranting natural consequences. This was all-out defiance that required a carefully placed and well-thought-out swat or two, according to Jim's and my agreement.

So I prayed for courage. *This is for her good*, I kept reminding myself. I explained to her what I was doing and why, then found the flyswatter (which stings but doesn't injure). A few minutes after the spanking, I took Abby on my lap, hugged her, and told her I loved her, which was why I cared how she behaved. I cried more tears than she did. But it helped establish trust, respect, and a more hands-on relationship between us. Abby learned she could trust me to do what I said I would do, even in the area of discipline. It was a defining moment.

Jim and I continued the same philosophy of natural consequences for childish irresponsibility and a swat for willful defiance with each of our children. It never got easier, but I grew more confident, knowing that "all discipline for the moment seems not to be joyful, but sorrowful; yet to those who have been trained by it, afterwards it yields the peaceful fruit of righteousness" (Hebrews 12:11, NASB). That was what we were going for, after all.

One of the hardest areas for a stepmom is discipline. Thank goodness for the relationship experts who offered this encouraging advice:

- When, as a stepmother, you have to enforce a rule already in place, "you may feel guilty, bad, abusive, hated, isolated, overwhelmed, and unloved. Hang on to the boundary!"[1] write Drs. Henry Cloud and John Townsend in *Boundaries with Kids*. This can be difficult, even for a biological parent. But remember you are loving this child and doing what is best for him or her. Stay strong!

- "Don't make empty threats. Follow up on promised consequences. That's where your true power resides. You can't make a child behave, but you can structure choices and consequences that help the child choose rightly,"[2] Cloud and Townsend continue.

- "Few things are more important in the blended family than the parents being committed to consistency in enforcing the consequences,"[3] writes Gary Chapman in *The Five Love Languages of Teenagers*.

Discipline is tough. It's challenging enough for intact families. But it's especially tough for stepfamilies—tough on kids who shuffle between homes with different rules, tough for parents and stepparents to agree on how to discipline, tough to decide which actions guarantee which consequences, tough to follow through. Whole volumes have been written on discipline, and as stepmoms, we're still not always sure what to do. No wonder so many stepmothers shudder or shut down at the very mention of the word.

Yet according to an article in *Christianity Today*, "Half of all children in the U.S. will have a stepparent during their lifetime, and 40 percent of women are predicted to either be a stepparent or be married to one at some point."[4] So as much as we may cringe at the thought of disciplining stepchildren, we must deal with it. It reminds me of our stepmom version of the *Mission: Impossible* tape introducing a new mission assignment: "Your mission, stepmom, should you choose to accept it, is to lead and guide your kids and stepkids through the turbulent waters of their childhood and adolescence. That is the true meaning of discipline—to train. Do not think of discipline merely as punishment. This tape will self-destruct in five seconds. You, however, need to stay strong. Good luck, stepmom."

When it comes to discipline, it can feel as if you have been given an impossible mission to perform, but there really are just a few key points to remember. After that, you need to figure out what best suits your family and situation, often by trial and error. And you can always read some of those volumes dedicated to discipline.

If you have kids who travel back and forth between homes, try to coordinate with the kids' other parent or stepparent so the rules and consequences are as consistent as possible. This would happen in a perfect world. But since "perfect" doesn't describe any of our situations, then you will have to do the best you can and not worry too much about it. Remember, "good enough" is not a cop-out. It is not settling. Good enough truly can be good enough. So please stop worrying. Worrying won't help. Instead, try these helpful tips:

- Seasoned stepmoms advise giving kids at least thirty minutes' reentry time to adjust to being in your home after having been at the other parent's home (or grandparents'). Don't immediately bombard them with questions, assignments, or general chatter.
- Remember, your stepkids may not always react the same way each time you instruct or advise them. They have bad moods and bad days just like you do. Cut them some slack.

- Make it as easy as possible for your stepkids to obey. Make sure the rules and consequences are clear, age appropriate, and reasonable. Let the biological parent take the lead in explaining how this will work and what it will look like.
- If biological children and stepchildren are living in the same house, and their parents have different expectations for their behavior and responsibilities, this can lead to conflict. Don't be afraid of it. It's normal.
- "Conflict will always be inevitable and conflict resolution will always be difficult,"[5] writes author and professor Dr. Mike Moore. Don't let the conflict scare you away from the standards you and your children's/stepchildren's other parents have set for them. It's just part of our—and their—reality.

Discipline in a stepfamily requires a lot of letting go, mostly of your own ideas of control. Realize that you have no control over what happens in the other home. If your rules are different from the rules in your children's/stepchildren's other home, don't expect them to follow your rules in the other home, and don't get angry with them if they don't. What if the kids are allowed to engage in certain activities at the other home that they are not permitted to engage in at your home? Provided those activities aren't illegal, that's just something else you can't control.

If you find out illegal activities are going on and it concerns your biological child, then you have a right and a responsibility to address the situation with your child's other biological parent. If it concerns your stepchild, discuss it with your husband (your stepchild's biological father) and let him take the lead in dealing with the situation. And remember to pray. Always pray. You may have to deal with the consequences later, but again, that's all you can do. And it's good enough.

Eleven-year-old Jason spends time in four homes—his biological mother and stepfather's, his biological father and stepmother's, his maternal grandparents', and his paternal grandparents'. Each of them has different rules. When he was younger, Jason would often get confused and frustrated trying to keep them all straight. Now he remembers the rules but tries to "get away with" actions at one home that he knows wouldn't fly in another, and it often gets him in trouble. One day at Grandpa's house (the house with the strictest rules), Grandpa put his arm around Jason and sat down beside him on the sofa.

"Jason, it must get confusing trying to keep track of all the different rules at all the different houses you go to." Jason nodded in agreement. "Grandpa has an idea that just might help you," his grandfather continued. "Would you agree that Grandpa has the strictest rules?" Again Jason nodded. "Well, what if you just followed Grandpa's rules at each house? Then you wouldn't have so much to remember, and you wouldn't get in trouble. Wouldn't you like to do that?"

Jason thought about it a moment, considering all the pros and cons, remembering what he could do somewhere else that he couldn't do at Grandpa's.

"Nope," he said. And with that, he jumped down from the sofa, and off he ran. Try as you might, when there are many people making decisions regarding how to raise a child, sometimes you will have to accept your limitations, stepmom.

Remember, there is more than one effective way to parent, and when it comes to the different ages and personalities of your kids and stepkids, discipline might look different for each one and will certainly change over the years. In stepparenting, you don't have the luxury of providing the only input into your children's or stepchildren's training. This is another area where you have to release them to God and trust Him with the outcome. You can do it, stepmom!

While I (Kathi) agree in principle with the experts who say that it's up to the parent—not the stepparent—to discipline, there are some instances where you'll need to step in and dole out immediate consequences. This is when a list of rules can be very helpful. For one thing, the kids know the house rules and understand your expectations. Also, it's so important for you and your spouse to be on the same page when it comes to discipline. Discuss the following questions with your spouse and spend some time coming up with guidelines for disciplining your children and stepchildren:

- Who will handle the discipline?
- How can I back you up if you are disciplining your child?
- How do you want me to handle discipline if you're not home?
- How is it best for me to talk to you when I think we need to talk about discipline? (Should I call you at work? Wait until you get home? Bring it up after dinner?)

STEPSIBLING ATTRACTION

Kathi and I (Carol) both know from stories and research that a potential mine field for any stepfamily involves sexual attraction between stepsiblings, including those of the same sex. Parents and stepparents often react with shock to the possibility, thinking it couldn't happen in their family, and ignore the dangers. Please don't let that happen to you. Be aware. Be proactive.

It's natural for hormonally charged, biologically unrelated teens and preteens to be attracted to each other. They don't share DNA, which experts say contributes to the incest taboo that blood-related siblings usually experience. They're being encouraged to develop close ties with their new family members and they can be confused about their thoughts and feelings. They live in the sexually charged atmosphere of "newlyweds" (you, their parents).

A few guidelines up front can help protect you, your children,

and stepchildren from this heartache. Counselors suggest the following strategies:

From your stepfamily's first days, talk to your teens and preteens
about your new living situation, including the possibility of developing attractions. Be open and honest, allowing them to express their
thoughts and feelings. Speak matter-of-factly. Let the kids know they
can talk with you about anything, including actions and circumstances
that make them uncomfortable. Embarrassing or not, stick with the
conversation. Let your teens and preteens know that you as parents
have chosen boundaries for your home designed to ensure everyone's
health, safety, and comfort. Even if your rules seem unnecessary to the
kids, make sure everyone understands—and follows—them. You can
explain that part of your job is protecting your kids and family, and this
is a big part of that. As the stepmom, you can expect some pushback on
this from older kids, but stick to your principles. The welfare of your
family depends on it.

When developing your guidelines, consider how you want to handle such everyday (yet potentially explosive) issues as bedroom and
bathroom privacy, lounging on the sofa or bed while talking or watching television, storage of personal care items in a shared bathroom, and
laundering lingerie and pajamas. You also may want to consider how
to monitor the sexual content of movies and television shows allowed
in your home, as well as topics of conversation that may lead to inappropriate sharing.

Some ideas to consider for your family policy include not being
alone with people of the opposite sex (or the same sex if an attraction
exists) in a bedroom; knocking before entering a closed door; wearing
clothing that fits and covers body parts; behaving toward non-biological
members of the stepfamily as weekend guests, which includes only fra-
ternal physical contact during swimming or other sports; and deciding

who stays home alone with whom. (You might have a list of rules that is posted somewhere in the hall/bathroom for guidelines regarding dress, showers, and so on, for everyone. Make sure that you and your husband are following those same rules.)

As the biological parent, in private, talk to your child about God's plan for human sexuality and how following it honors ourselves and others, and provides us with the protection and pleasure He intended. As part of this discussion, include the normalcy of attraction to others (including the possibility of stepsiblings) and how to act during those times. Counselors advise being careful not to shame them or instill fear, but to empower them with information regarding their sexuality. As part of this conversation, be sure to let them know how males react to visual stimulation and encourage—and model—modest dress by everyone in your home. It's all part of honoring and respecting each other.

Be sure to keep the words and tone age-appropriate. And as one more word to the wise, counselors recommend realizing the danger of attraction between fathers and non-biological daughters, and staying aware of red flags.

If lines have already been crossed? Seek counseling immediately, both as a family and for the individuals involved. Beware of overreacting and shaming.

Roger and I (Kathi) talked about this issue before we got married since we would have three teenagers living with us: my daughter, my son, and Roger's son. Complicating the fact of a new blended family was the close quarters we would all be living in: five people in less than 1300 square feet. All the kids shared one bathroom.

One of the biggest factors that helped all of us through this living situation was modesty. Both Roger and I are pretty modest people and our kids have taken on that trait. Roger and I always dressed as if we had overnight guests whenever we were out of our bedroom (sweats or a robe over pajamas). We didn't have to ask our kids to cover up; they did so naturally. We insisted all the kids use "dorm rules": When you walk to the bathroom, wear your pajamas, and always come out of the restroom fully dressed.

Another thing that made the situation easier was that Roger and I would have regular conversations with our own kids about their comfort level. If one of the kids was doing something that made another child uncomfortable, we wanted to know.

At one point, one of our kids came to us to let us know that another child's friend made them uncomfortable. We decided to stop allowing that friend to spend the night. Going forward, if a child wanted a friend to spend the night, that child and their friend slept in the living room, and the child who didn't have an overnight guest got their room all to themselves. These "house rules" were established to help protect our kids. Our best advice? Talk through these issues before you get married. Already married? It's not too late. You would much rather deal with this issue in the abstract than when a line has been crossed.

LIFE INSURANCE

This was the second awkward conversation Roger and I (Kathi) had while we were engaged. (The first was when I, the woman with huge debt and no assets, offered to sign a prenup so Roger wouldn't have to ask. He politely declined.) Right before we got married, we went over all our finances. When we got to life insurance, Roger went to change the beneficiary to me. But what if we both died? I would've understood if Roger had reservations about putting my kids on his policy. After all, he'd already put twenty years in at his job, and I was bringing almost nothing of financial worth to the table. Roger wanted to put all four kids on the policy. He wasn't concerned about what was "fair" as much as he was about making sure all of our kids still had a relationship with each other if something happened to us.

Every family needs to decide what will work for them. Perhaps one of your exes also has a life insurance policy. Will that affect the amount you give to the other kids whose parent doesn't have a policy? Will the ages and stages of your kids influence the amount? What if you or your spouse passes away before the other? How will the money be distributed then? These are all essential things to talk about and understand before a crisis hits. Some larger companies have great human resource departments that can help you think through these issues and make the best decisions for your stepfamily.

WILLS

When Roger and I (Kathi) first got married, wills weren't something we ever discussed. Perhaps when you were first married, you too were just scraping by, and the thought of talking about inheritance seemed as far-fetched as talking about whom you were going to pass your royal title down to. But as the years went by, you may have paid off some bills, acquired a house and a couple of cars, made some investments, and generally become more, well, grown up.

Nonblended families have come to blows over this kind of stuff. So think of how important it is in a blended-family situation to get your will made out properly. Regarding blended-family situations, most experts don't recommend that you leave everything to the surviving spouse; instead they advise spelling out in advance the wishes you both have and then specifying those in the will. (Roger and I also have "In Case I Die" folders on each of our computers that contain all the "stuff" the other spouse needs to know if something should happen to either of us.)

I'm not here to give legal advice, but the best relationship advice I can give you is this: Write down your wishes. It will keep your stepkids from feeling like you're taking something from them that their dad wanted them to have, whether it's money, heirlooms, or photographs, and having clear-cut instructions will help to maintain the relationships long after the sterling-silver saltshaker has been doled out.

STUFF

Recently, while I (Kathi) was visiting my mom, she pointed out a few milk glass containers and said, "Hey, if I kick the bucket, don't just throw those out. They're worth something." Yep. That's my mom. Supersentimental, right?

Okay, so maybe *how* she said it was a bit earthy, but *what* she said was very valuable to me. I knew she was telling me, "There's a lot of stuff around here you don't have to worry about, but, hey, pay attention to the milk glass."

One of the best gifts we can give our kids is a *lack* of junk. I've written a lot on organization, and again and again women tell me about the legacy of "stuff" their parents and stepparents left to them—which, in many cases, is an overwhelming amount of possessions they have to sort through, not knowing what is of value, what is sentimental, what is important, and what is junk.

Keep a list of possessions that have value (either monetary or sentimental) and what you want to do with them. Then give your kids and stepkids the freedom to get rid of all the other stuff the way they see fit after you're gone. If you want your fabric collection to go to your favorite quilting group, great. Write that down and give your kids the current contact information of group members to connect with them.

Many adult children have been stuck with so much of their parents' or stepparents' stuff that it becomes like another person living in their home. They feel paralyzed by indecision. And the guilt over what to do seems to double when it's a stepparent's stuff.

Before Roger and I were married, a man who had fallen on hard times lived with Roger for a few months. This was more than twelve years ago, and the man left stuff at Roger's house. We have no way of contacting him and have no idea where he is or who is in contact with him. Every time I get the nerve to get rid of his things, I can't do it. There are picture albums, an old Bible, and more. I'm sure this is exactly how some people feel about getting rid of their parents' or step-parents' stuff. The man's stuff isn't serving any purpose at the moment, but I also cannot assume what is important to him and what isn't.

Don't leave your kids or stepkids with that burden.

CARS

Roger and I (Kathi) went into our marriage with two different thoughts on vehicles. His thought: Buy the kids their own car when they get their license and let them haul their own tushies to school and whatnot. My thought: Let them earn the money for their own cars. The compromise? We would match what they saved for up to a certain amount, as long as they bought the car outright. (We are believers in the Dave Ramsey approach to cars. My last car was a new car, but that was fifteen years ago; that's the last "new" car I will ever own. I don't ever want to make car payments again.)

Was it a compromise? Yes. But one we could both live with in the end.

Roger did go back to his kids and reset their expectations about cars. (He'd never told the kids he would buy them a car, but there had been innuendo to that effect.) One of the things we've both had to learn is that just because something was "the plan" five years ago doesn't mean it's the plan today.

Our kids, our exes, and we ourselves need to realize that sometimes plans have to change. Roger put a lot of thought into resetting his kids' expectations. But his philosophy is that things change, and we all have to reset expectations as our family deals with change.

MEDICAL BILLS AND INSURANCE

Who is going to pay the medical bills for your spouse's kids? For your kids? For you? This especially needs to be determined before the first big crisis comes up. This is one of the areas where "equal" has to go out the window, because you have to do whatever is best for the kids, and sometimes that means it isn't "fair." For most of our (Roger and Kathi's) marriage, all of our kids have been solely on our policy.

Fortunately we had Roger's insurance, and within the past few years, my ex had coverage through his work for my kids. But the paperwork was a nightmare, and exes aren't always easy to deal with. But recently we had a victory in this area. It turns out that my kids' dad covered them, but it cost significantly more than it would for us to cover them under Roger's plan. The good news is that we were able to come to an understanding (through e-mail—remember—always through e-mail) where Roger still carries the kids on his insurance, but their dad is paying all the copays. It's a win for us, a win for my ex, and a win for the kids. It doesn't always work out that all three can win, but when it does, that's something to celebrate!

TALKING WITH HIS EX

So much of what we have to decide regarding stepstuff also involves our spouse's ex-wife. And those can be tough conversations to have. They can be emotionally taxing and hard on everyone involved. In those stressful situations, people often hear—or don't hear—what they want to. So how do you handle tough conversations with your spouse's ex?

Recently I (Kathi) met an elementary-school teacher who'd been in the biz for more than twenty years. I always love to hear tricks of the trade and what makes people successful. I asked her what her best piece of advice was when it came to being a teacher. Her response? E-mail.

I pressed her a little bit more, and here is what she had to say:

"I used to talk to parents on the phone, and it seemed that every time there was a misunderstanding. Finally I went totally to e-mail. I'm required by the school to have a phone line, so in my outgoing message, I state that I don't return phone calls and to please e-mail me at _____. Having everything in writing when you're talking to distraught parents who may or may not have all the facts from their kids has saved me a world of hurt.

"Also, I have someone I team-teach with, and anytime I have a parent conference in my room, we open the dividing wall so that the other teacher can hear everything that is going on. It's great to have a third party who can hear both sides of the conversation so that if I don't make something clear, or if the parents mishear something, I have someone I can rely on to help me straighten it out. Also, parents are a lot more reasonable when they know that someone else is listening to their conversation."

I learned a few things about communicating with my husband's ex from listening to this teacher's wise advice:

1. *When the situation is combative, e-mail is better than voice mail.* We've covered this before, but it's a good reminder. It's great to have a paper trail to keep track of who said what, and this isn't just to keep the other party honest. Many times I've agreed to something in the moment in person or on the phone and then forgotten what I said later on. E-mail not only keeps a paper trail; it gives me time to check schedules, think through what's best for my husband and the kids, and talk it over with my guy. Sometimes in the heat of the moment, I may not always say what I want to say, or say it in a way that is loving. But with e-mail, I have time to think, pray, and respond in the way I would want to for my stepkids.

2. *I may just be the crazy one.* I have been known to be unreasonable and emotional. I want to be a godly woman in every aspect of my life, and I don't get a pass when I'm talking to my husband's ex-wife.

3. *Three are better than two.* When there is a third party in the room, all of us tend to be on our best behavior. In my first marriage, which was very combative, our therapist suggested that if we fought, we should fight on the front porch, since we'd never want our neighbors to hear us raising our voices to each other. (It's sad that sometimes we didn't feel the same way about our own children.) So when it comes to communicating with my spouse's ex, having a third person around ensures that I'm demonstrating self-control.

Remember what I said earlier about our stepkids seeing who we are? Our spouse's ex forms opinions about us as well. We can't control what they think about us, of course, but we can control what we show them. When we use self-control and grace in our words and actions, when we're being intentional about how we communicate, we're teaching our kids and stepkids what it looks like to treat others with respect, even when it's hard. It's worth the effort, stepmom!

SIX

Define Your Role: Mom, Martyr, or Minister?

She speaks with wisdom, and faithful

instruction is on her tongue.

—PROVERBS 31:26

Carol

I couldn't believe what I was hearing. Then I couldn't believe I was arguing with a voice on the radio. "You have got to be kidding me," I said, emphasizing every word. When I first heard a well-known radio psychologist say that stepmothers have no meaningful role in the family, it blew me away. I wondered if she only studied statistics and stereotypes, not actual stepmothers. "No meaningful role"—really?

I used to be a newspaper reporter, and I wonder about a lot of things. I also like to ask a lot of questions. Some people consider it a little bit nosey, but I consider it intellectual curiosity. I find out a lot this way. And I've found out from observing and talking to lots of stepmothers that we make *huge* contributions to our families.

And so I wondered if Famous Radio Psychologist was missing a key point in her analysis. Or perhaps she misspoke. Maybe she meant to say "no *clear-cut* role," because heaven knows, that is certainly true.

Either way, rather than buying into the radio speaker's statement,

I agree with Beth Moore when she writes in *Get Out of That Pit*, "[God is] up to something big that affects not only you, but those around you."[1]

Even more important than what anyone else believes is what *you* believe. And it's equally important *you* believe that what *you* do in your stepfamily matters. Let me tell you what I believe: Your stepchildren are beyond blessed to have you in their lives. True statement. It doesn't matter if they don't know it or believe it just yet, but it sure matters that *you* believe it. Because what you believe determines how you behave.

I know not everyone (your stepchildren, their biological moms, Famous Radio Psychologist, possibly even you) agrees with me on this point, and that's okay. But hear me out. When the Spirit of the living God resides in you, the same Spirit that raised Jesus Christ from the dead (Romans 8:11), girlfriend, people are blessed to even *know* you, much less get to live with you.

Even if you aren't yet a Christian, you bring many strengths to your stepfamily, and let's face it, you rock! Just the fact that you would take on a role of this magnitude and want to do it well when, as one stepmom said, all you really wanted was a husband, makes you a hero.

Keep this in mind. I know it can be a struggle—especially on those days when the stepkids hurl accusations in your face or treat you like a leper, and others question your value—to believe you are a blessing. But it is truth, and we need to constantly remind ourselves of it, because at any given moment, we not only have no idea what to do, but we don't even know who we are in this relationship. Everybody (our husband, the kids, their biological mom) has a different opinion. And if we have more than one stepchild, our role can differ with each one *at the same time.*

We wonder, are we to act like babysitters? Referees? Fairy godmothers? Battlefield generals?

"A Kiss from God"

Stacey viewed her role as a stepmom to three-year-old Betsy and seven-year-old Daniel as a mission "to come into this very difficult position and contribute to the well-being of these children."

So she did. For the eight years she was married to their father, she committed herself to do her best, before God, to love them. For eight years she received zero positive response from the boy. Zip. Nada. He called her his stepmonster. He tried twice to harm her newborn. (Stacey got Daniel into counseling to learn new coping skills, and she kept a close watch.) Betsy, however, responded to Stacey's overtures. They developed a close, loving relationship.

Even after Stacey and the kids' father divorced, she kept in touch with them, remembering their birthdays with cards and cupcakes, giving them Christmas gifts, attending their games and graduations. Betsy loves Stacey and includes her in family activities. Betsy's children call her Grandma Stacey. For more than twenty-five years, Daniel never responded to the same demonstrations of love Stacey showed to both him and his sister. Until recently.

At an extended-family gathering for Betsy's daughter's birthday, Stacey took turns roller skating with her current husband, her teenage son, and others at the party. For a moment, she found herself alone. When she looked up, Daniel was skating toward her. He reached her side, took her hand, led her around the rink—and kept skating. Stacey's heart pounded as they circled the rink, neither saying a word, neither daring to break the silence. When they finished skating, Daniel hugged her and skated off without a word, leaving Stacey alone at the rail.

"I know it was Daniel's way of saying, 'We're good. I appreciate you.' It was like a kiss from God, like God saying, 'You did okay.' Now when I see Daniel, he'll give me a hug, and it's warm." Then Stacey's voice trailed off. "After all those years . . ."

To a large degree, our role as stepmoms will be determined by the stepchildren themselves and what kind of relationship they want to have with us, as well as the relationship they will *allow* us to have with them. It can break your heart for a stepchild to reject the love you want to give, but even if this happens, keep on keepin' on. Keep on working at building trust. Fluid and flexible, that's you. Determined. Committed. Brave. And full of hope.

"Betsy adores me. Daniel couldn't stand me for years. Which one defines me? Neither, because I always tried to do the right thing before God," Stacey told us.

And that defines a *successful* stepmom. You can be a successful stepmom too. We have the freedom to adapt the role to fit whatever best serves our families at any given time. We're awesome that way.

It's Not Personal

Remember the opening line of *The Purpose-Driven Life*, Rick Warren's best seller? "It's not about you."[2] For stepmoms, that's a good way to say, "Don't take things personally." As in Stacey's case, a lot of the frustrations and irritations you may experience in your role are not directed at *you*, wonderful person that you are, but at you *the stepmom*. A lot of the issues swirling around stepfamily life just are what they are, and it's a lengthy process to decipher and work through them. But you can.

Children in certain life stages are more open to adult input than at other times. A basic knowledge of child development helps here. It's usually easier for younger children to accept you, while teens will make you earn their respect. Remember, too, that teens are naturally becoming more independent and want to spread their wings, while you want to pull everyone close and cement family ties.

And speaking of teenagers, I read in a magazine years ago one psychologist's recommendation that we remember teenagers should "be treated as outpatients from a mental institution. They can function, but they're not all there." It can help you understand how *at the same time,* one stepchild may treat you like a confidante, one may treat you like a big sister, and another may treat you like the plague.

A HIGH CALLING

Nonetheless, being a stepmother is a "high calling," Christian counselor and stepmom Jennifer Cecil of Phoenix, Arizona, shares with us. It helps to keep a spiritual perspective on it, too, she adds. "It calls us higher. It sharpens us. God put me in this position. He has chosen me to impart something to [these kids]. I asked God to help me lay down my life for [them]. I prayed, 'God, what do You want me to do?'"

Given their usually high anger level (and their inexperience in dealing with that anger), their immaturity, and their typical moodiness, how teenage stepchildren think and feel about you today may not be how they think and feel about you tomorrow. The status can change from one day to the next . . . and from one *moment* to the next. It's only one of a stepmom's many surprises when it comes to dealing with teens. Let's take a look at seven other surprises you might encounter:

1. The amount of anger. "You can almost bet that everyone in a blended family is mad at someone or someone is mad at them,"[3] writes Dr. Kevin Leman in *Living in a Step-Family Without Getting Stepped On.*

2. The fact that stepkids often miss their "old" family, even if it involved neglect or abuse.

3. How long it takes to transition into a blended family. Experts say from three to five years. Hang in there.

4. Not feeling instant love for your stepchildren. No need for guilt. Be diligent and intentional about showing love, regardless of your feelings.

5. Just how unrealistic your expectations really were regarding blending families or stepparenting.
6. How guilty you feel. Guilty your previous marriage failed. Guilty a divorce meant no full-time father for your children. Guilty for disrupting your children's lives. Guilty your children have to adjust to a stepfamily. Guilty because your stepchildren reject you. Guilty because you are not perfect.
7. How hard it is.

One stepmom told me she was so disappointed because her stepchildren treated her like . . . well, like a stepmom. She *felt* like their mother. She thought of the children as hers and treated them as such. But as much as they liked her and as well as they got along, they already had a mother, and it wasn't her.

Important Conversations

I remember reading books with five-year-old Abby a few months before marrying Jim. We took turns reading aloud. After a while I rested my eyes and listened to her breeze through a book about a circus animal. "The crowd broke into applesauce," she said. My eyes popped open.

"Applesauce? Let's look at that word again."

"Ohhhhh," she exclaimed. "Applause!" We both smiled.

"That sounds better, doesn't it?" I said.

After reading, our conversation turned to memories, including some of her mother. I wanted her to be comfortable with me, to know we could talk about anything together. Abby's mother had been my close friend before she passed away. I told Abby about my being at the hospital the night Abby was born, about what a beautiful baby she was, and how thankful everyone was for her safe delivery.

We talked about the time I joined Abby, Jim, and Cathy on a camping trip in the Arizona mountains when Abby was two. Jim, of course, did all the work while Cathy, Abby, and I relaxed, making s'mores around the campfire. Abby and I laughed and remembered all of us marching in a Vacation Bible School parade led by a giant mechanical bull on loan from a car dealership. The parade included people dressed up as chocolate, vanilla, and strawberry milkshakes!

It seemed like a good time to make a point. I wanted Abby to know that while I would be in the *position* of mom after her dad and I married, and I would think of myself that way, I knew her first mom would always be special to her. I had no intention of trying to take Cathy's place. We would each have our own place in Abby's life and heart.

"I know you love your mother very much, and I'm glad you do. I loved her too. She was my good friend. We both miss her," I said, pushing her dark hair back from her eyes.

"Is it okay if I love you, too?" she asked.

"I would like it if you did. I love you," I answered.

"But I love her more."

"That's okay. You don't have to feel the same way about me that you do about your mother. God gives us lots of different kinds of love for all the people in our lives."

"Would Mom mind if I love you?"

"Your mom would be happy to know you have love in your heart for everyone in your family. It doesn't take love away from her for you to love me. God just keeps adding more love to our hearts." (This thought also came in handy later when we welcomed Baby Allison and then Baby Andrea to our family.)

"You're kind of like Mom and kind of not like Mom," she answered.

"That's true," I said. "We're alike in some ways and different in other ways. That's good. Each person is special. You're not exactly like anyone else either. God made each of us special, and that's good."

(Note: Even if open hostility characterizes the current relationship with your stepchildren, you can aim to communicate the bottom line:

That you are not here to replace anyone. You are here to be yourself, and you are available to them. You are *not* here to be abused, neglected, or ignored, however.)

As Abby got older, conversations could get a little more difficult to navigate. Let me share one we had when she was twelve. Now I know just being twelve can be reason enough for *a mood*, but everything irritated Abby that day: the care her teeth required in braces, the doctor's orders to eliminate certain favorite foods to check for an allergy and my insistence she follow them, the antics of her two younger sisters. But it seemed like there was more going on that day. School matters, I asked? Issues with friends? And then I thought of one more thing.

"Does it seem strange having pictures of two moms in your room?"

"Yes," she answered. Her eyes, usually so full of life, swam in sadness. It broke my heart.

"I bet you miss her."

"Yes." Harder tears.

"I do too." Now my own tears started. Abby's tears stopped. Her eyes reflected a hint of surprise. Abby got up, came over, and gave me a hug.

Gaining control of myself, I asked, "Do you think she would make you brush and floss and follow the doctor's orders too? I bet she would."

Abby stared at me.

"I'm not being mean, you know, when I make you do those things. It's because I love you. I want you to have healthy teeth and for your tummy to feel better."

Abby continued to stare.

"Do you feel different because you have two moms?"

"No. Lots of kids have more than one mom, and some don't have any parents at all."

"That's a good point. I want you to remember a few things. Remember you are twelve, and feelings can get weird at times. Remember

I love you. Sometimes I have to make you do hard things, things you don't want to do. But remember, it doesn't mean I don't love you. Actually, it's because I *do* love you."

And then I thought of one more thing.

"Is there something that would say 'love' to you that I'm missing?"

"Yes."

"What is it?" I asked, heart trembling.

"Staying up until nine." Now her eyes sparkled.

"Well, I'll talk to Dad about that after he gets home."

Whew.

As moms and stepmoms, we have to tread carefully when it comes to our kids' and stepkids' emotions. We need to look past the surface to try to see where the hurt is really stemming from. And sometimes, like that day with Abby, it helps to listen and show how much we care.

TWO MOMS

Sometimes a stepmom *can* be a real mom. God can bond hearts without a bloodline. Some situations (like mine, when the mother of a young child has died) more naturally lend themselves to it and grow toward it. Others don't. Don't worry about it. You don't have total control over that, either. Relationships don't depend on only one person.

It's a good idea to tell stepchildren, in an age-appropriate manner, your intentions to be there for them but not come between them and their mother. Giving your stepchildren permission to love and be loyal to their biological mother (even if she is serving time in the state pen as an ax murderer) is kind and wise and reflects well on you. This is true whether their mother is alive or dead.

Christian counselor and stepmom Deborah Tyrrell took it one step further. She wrote a letter to her stepchild's biological mother, affirming her in her role and congratulating her on the job she had done rearing her daughter. Tyrrell let her know she was there to support her stepdaughter's parents in their role, not compete for the affection of their daughter. Soon after, Tyrrell noticed a shift in her stepdaughter's attitude toward her.

"She felt pulled," Tyrrell told us. "If she liked me, it felt like she was being disloyal to her mom."

When Tyrrell's stepdaughter and her mom both knew they had no reason to feel threatened, it gave her stepdaughter permission to like Tyrrell. And soon she did. Sometimes children will idealize a parent who has died or left, imagining him or her never losing patience, never getting angry, never making them do anything they don't want to do. Usually time and maturity bring them back to reality.

Speak Their Language

Like my conversation with Abby, it helps to know what says *love* to our stepchildren. One way is to learn their love languages, what specifically speaks to them and fills their "love tanks." Dr. Gary Chapman's best-selling book *The Five Love Languages*[4] goes into great detail on how to discover and express love the way people best receive it—their love language. He describes the love languages as quality time, words of affirmation, gifts, acts of service, and physical touch. Check out your love languages and those of your stepfamily members in that book, as well as Chapman's *The Five Love Languages of Teenagers*[5] and *The Five Love Languages of Children*,[6] coauthored by Chapman and Dr. Ross Campbell.

Lots of factors influence how your stepchildren view your role and how they relate to you. Their current ages, their ages at the time of your marriage to their father, their temperaments, and how well their temperaments react with yours are just a few. Some personalities just click better than others.

WHICH ONE ARE YOU?

Check out your basic stepmother tendencies. Depending on your personality, you may naturally be more inclined to be the fun stepmom, the bossy stepmom, the "whatever" stepmom, or the "poor, pitiful me" stepmom—with all the strengths and weaknesses of each. Learn your own tendencies and then take steps to highlight the ones that help you connect with your stepkids, and correct the ones that bring you and your stepchildren down. Kathi and I will give you plenty of ideas in this book to help in every way we can.

Which of the following best describes your current stepmom persona?

- *Fun stepmom.* If we don't stick to the rules (or the schedule or the budget or the eating plan), it's okay. It's more important to bond over the fun of this moment. Plus, the kids will love me and think I'm a delight. Strength: You generally enjoy life and see the humor in things. You are fun to be around, and people like you. Weakness: You can tend to be a tad irresponsible by valuing fun above all. Stepchildren can easily manipulate you to avoid responsibilities and can wind up losing respect for you.
- *Bossy stepmom.* These kids need shaping up, and they will do what I say. I'm the adult here, and they will respect me. Strength: You get things done. You know what needs to be done and who needs to do it. Weakness: You can appear controlling and can put people off by your "my way or the highway" style. Stepchildren can resent this approach and dig in their heels. This is usually where the "You're not my real mom. You can't tell me what to do!" screams come from.
- *"Whatever" stepmom.* Yeah, "whatever." Strength: You are easygoing and take things in stride. Nothing much disturbs

you. Weakness: You can appear uninterested at times. Stepchildren can interpret this as lack of concern and care and
return the vibe.

- *"Poor, pitiful me" stepmom.* I can't believe how these kids have
  been allowed to behave. I can't believe I have to live with
  them now. I can't believe nobody appreciates *how hard* my
  job is, and what a good job I do. I can't believe . . . You get
  the picture. Strength: You are sensitive to all the adjustments
  required by everyone in your stepfamily. You appreciate all
  the effort to make this work. Weakness: You see yourself as a
  victim and can easily start to resemble a martyr. Who wants
  to be around that?

And Dinner, Too?

In the early days, I tended toward being the fun stepmom, wanting to
establish trust and a strong connection as soon as possible, spending
our summer days bonding over coloring books, games of Candy Land,
and Amy Grant albums. Abby and I acted out endless scenes with her
favorite Strawberry Shortcake dolls. One evening Jim came home from
work to find Abby and me sprawled on the living room floor reading
an Amelia Bedelia book (who just happens to have the same initials as
Abby Boley). After his customary hug and kiss of greeting, he asked
the obvious question.

"What's for dinner?"

"I'm not sure yet," I cheerily replied. "We've been reading and having fun all day." I thought he would be proud of the way I had spent
my time, building connection with Abby. He was.

"Glad you had a fun day," he said. But he was also hungry. So it
made perfect sense when he added, "And can we have dinner, too?"

Oh yes, dinner. And clean laundry. We also needed that. Obviously

I needed to discipline my time management a bit more rigorously if I hoped to teach Abby the same thing. Perhaps the next day Abby and I could bond by tossing a salad and folding some clothes, along with Amelia Bedelia, of course.

STEPMOM STRONG

Stepmoms, I salute you. Your courage and determination inspire me. Come eavesdrop on some stories stepmothers have told me about their influence on their stepfamilies. Some may sound a lot like your own.

- Tiffany said she was the one who listened reflectively without judging, letting her stepchildren express their feelings and figure things out for themselves without being told what they "should" do.
- Brittany told me she taught her stepchildren to say "please" and "thank you" and even to take a daily shower.
- Gabrielle said she was the one who introduced her stepchildren to Jesus. Does it get more meaningful than that?

SECRETS FOR SUCCESS

How did these stepmoms do it? They shared a few secrets for stepmom success:

- Believe you are a valuable gift to your family.
- Keep building into their lives, even if they don't respond.
- Stay flexible, adjusting to fit the needs of your stepfamily.
- Think of yourself as an adult in your stepchildren's lives who cares about them and their welfare, who can step back emotionally, listen objectively, and offer insight.
- Picture your role as that of an aunt, an adult in the family with a position of authority, but a step down from a mother.

- Or imagine yourself as a coach, a camp counselor, a Girl Scout leader.
- Realize you have the possibility, over time, to become a trusted confidante.

But it won't happen overnight. Be patient not only with your stepchildren but with yourself as well. It takes awhile for everyone to get their bearings, accept and adjust to change, and build trust.

Give children plenty of time to get to know you for the wonderful person you are. It is perfectly normal for a stepchild to reject a stepmother. It wouldn't matter if you were Mother Teresa or Lady Gaga.

How to Love Your Stepkids When You Don't Even Like Them

So you want to be a thoughtful, loving stepmother, but the feelings just aren't there? What if you don't even *like* your stepchildren?

First, be assured your feelings, or lack of them, are normal and won't qualify you as a "wicked" stepmother. Feelings do not define us, nor are they the boss of us. When stepchildren hurl accusations at us, resent us, won't make eye contact with us, or call us "her," it's normal not to experience warm, fuzzy feelings toward them. We can be tempted to feel guilty and ashamed of that, but Jesus doesn't condemn us, and there is no need for us to either. It helps to know it is our *actions*, not our *feelings*, that matter most.

Psychologist Kevin Leman writes, "They [stepparents] are greatly relieved to hear that it is perfectly normal for a stepchild to reject a stepparent. And they are doubly relieved to hear that it's also normal if a stepparent doesn't love a stepchild with the same intensity he or she has for a natural child."[7]

Stepmothers who pressure themselves to feel love for their stepchildren often sabotage the process. Feelings are not the key.

"I thought I should be able to feel love for my husband's children just because they were his children," Phyllis said. "It relieved me of so much guilt to realize it was my actions and attitudes toward them that mattered."

God can use the lack of a biological bond to prompt the extra effort required to build a relationship with each stepchild. Don't worry if you don't feel about your stepchildren the way you think you *should*. As one stepmom said, "I don't know how to live with someone else's children, much less *love* them."

Although some stepmothers develop a genuine love and affection for their stepchildren, don't think there's anything wrong with you if you don't. An intense feeling of love for stepchildren may never come. That's okay. Keeping a child's best interests at heart and acting in loving ways represent the best of stepparenting.

FEELINGS—NOTHING MORE THAN FEELINGS

To help you act in spite of your feelings, or lack thereof, try the following suggestions, which have worked brilliantly for many stepmoms:

- First, as doctors swear in the Hippocratic Oath, "Do no harm." Life is hard enough as it is; we don't want to do or say anything to make it harder for ourselves or our stepkids.
- Act "as if" you feel loving. "It is the way to actually become more loving by acting ourselves into a different way of responding," write Tony Campolo and Mary Darling in *Connecting Like Jesus*.[8] This isn't being fake or hypocritical. It's being wise and doing the right thing by not letting your feelings dictate your behavior, something we hopefully started learning at approximately age two. One way to do this is through service. I learned that the Hebrew word for love, *ahav*, literally means "I give." Consider John 3:16, where Jesus

says that God "so loved" the world that "he gave." It is unselfish action that makes the difference. Jesus will help you do this.

- Remember to show basic courtesy. Psychologists tell us that feelings follow behavior. The more you behave in a certain way, the more your feelings start to follow suit. But even if they don't, it's still the right thing to do, and you can be proud of yourself for doing it.

- "Find healthy people you can vent to," suggests Christian counselor and stepmom Jennifer Cecil. "People who will encourage you." Christian counselor and stepmom Deborah Tyrrell adds, "Make sure it doesn't turn into a big bash party."[9] One stepmom said, "I have an ongoing support group of four women who hold me accountable and love me through the tough times." How wise.

- Be aware of your thoughts. Just as feelings follow behavior, behavior follows thought. Train yourself to look for the positive things about your stepkids, and guard your thoughts about them.

- Control your expressions, both on your face and in your voice. Every glance we cast sends a message, and that message packs a wallop. Expressions can set a mood, and children of all ages are sensitive to them. Smile at your stepchildren when they enter the room, even if they don't smile at you, or even look at you. Smile when you don't feel like smiling. No eye rolling or smirking. Model the behavior you want from them. We set the tone in our homes.

- Be the stepmom *you* want to be, not dependent on how others behave, think, or speak, either to or about you. Do not let others determine how you will behave. Don't give away your power. You're in charge of *you*. This is part of the message behind Jesus' command to turn the other cheek and go the extra mile—not to be a doormat, but to be in charge of your actions.

A friend of mine tells the story of Charlie, a resident in a nursing home. Charlie was restricted to a wheelchair and suffered constant and severe pain. Yet he always had a smile for the other residents and went out of his way to be thoughtful. When asked how he could be so pleasant in spite of his circumstances, Charlie replied, "Because that's the way I want to be."[10]

MISSIONARY STEPMOM

Imagine Jesus standing before you, arm around your stepchild, asking you to love this child for Him. At the same time He asks, He empowers you to do it. He gives you His own love to share with your stepchild. Remember, He said if you offer a glass of water in His name, He considers you did it for Him. And He and I both know you have done much more for this child than offer water.

"I'll do this for You, Jesus" turns being a stepmother into a ministry, making us missionaries to our own families. And like missionaries, we are doing something great for the kingdom of God. We are learning the language, customs, and culture of the "natives" and their territory and doing good works for them so we have the right to be heard. We are on a mission field, my friend, as surely as if we were traipsing through the jungles of Papua New Guinea. I know this is true because my daughter Andrea has done that very thing. And her stories of God at work, while amazing, are no more breathtaking than the ones many stepmothers share.

CODE NAME: STEPMOM

Sometimes we feel like Navy SEALs participating in covert operations. It can feel like we are behind enemy lines. After wading through all the uncertainty and insecurity, we complete our mission by following the orders of our Commanding Officer. Here is a healthy, practical, and scriptural way to define your role as a stepmother:

- I am intentional about showing love to each member of my stepfamily.
- I am a blessing to each member of my stepfamily. It doesn't matter whether they see it or not. Hopefully one day they will, but I can't control that.
- I am an example of how someone can experience peace and joy in the midst of some of life's toughest and most challenging circumstances.
- I am here to show my stepfamily how a godly woman lives, loves, gives, and forgives.
- I am here to show my stepfamily a woman secure in her God, her identity as His child, and her ability to be used by Him. He helps me with this.
- I am blessed as I bless others. I'm trusting God for this one.

How to set this in motion? Keep three priorities in order:

1. You are Jesus' beloved daughter.
2. You are your husband's wife.
3. You are a mother to any biological children, and you are a stepmother.

The following three steps, in this order, will help keep your purpose clear-cut and meaningful.

1. Center yourself in Christ and base your identity and worth in Him. As a bonus, when you focus on Christ, your family becomes the beneficiary.
2. Worship regularly with other believers. If you're part of a loving Christian community helping to meet the needs of others, it will seem more natural to take responsibility for the

nurture and care of children other than your own. All those summers you spent as a camp counselor? All those hours in the church nursery? They will pay off for you now.

3. Become involved in a care group or Sunday school class. This provides the opportunity for close relationships where you can share your struggles, receive prayer support, and know others love you just as you are. When you know you are loved, you can do great things.

Next to being Jesus' daughter, your top priority is being your husband's wife. This is your primary relationship in your stepfamily. Only part of that role is in support of him as his children's father. It's easy to get caught up in stepfamily drama and get distracted from your primary relationship. Don't let all of your conversations center around the children or your husband's ex. As one insightful stepmom said, "I don't want to have gone through all this and then have no husband!" Following are a few important ways to prioritize your marriage:

- Remember your commitment to your husband is for life, so aim to make the next fifty years or so as fun as possible. Deal with any leftover issues from the past so they don't destroy your marriage today or in the future. The airlines aren't the only place you will pay for extra baggage. Seek counseling, if necessary. Your marriage—and sanity—are worth it.

- Affirm your spouse in his roles as both a husband and a father/stepfather. Tell him when you see him doing an amazing job. Letting him know you're in his corner encourages him to be the best husband and dad/stepdad he can be. Compliment him often. Let him know you appreciate all he does for your stepfamily, and you know it's not easy for him.

- Stay aware. Privately, offer observations to your husband on his children's behavior (making sure not to criticize or condemn either the children or the poor job of discipline prior to your arrival on the scene) and welcome his perspective. Ask your husband how he thinks you can help meet his children's needs. Don't assume you know.

- Give him time alone with his kids.
- Ask him what he needs from you. Let him know your needs and how he can help meet them. He's not a mind reader. Then let him know he's your hero. These actions will endear you to him even more.

Finally, your priority is being a mother to any biological children and a stepmother to your husband's children. Maybe your biggest contribution to your stepfamily is living your consistently joyful life right there in front of them. Maybe your biggest contribution is listening without judging. Maybe your biggest contribution is showing them how to forgive and love people who don't always act in loving ways.

"You can be certain you are leaving a lasting legacy when you obey God because the most powerful way you influence people is leading them closer to Jesus,"[11] writes Dr. Charles Stanley. "When you demonstrate the character of Christ to others, your influence will be profound."

As a stepmother, you didn't give birth to your stepchildren, but you can give life to them. "No meaningful role" for stepmothers? No way. We've settled that argument. Of course there is. And you're playing it. Kathi and I believe you will do it well!

SEVEN

The Ex-Factor:
Accepting Your Stepkid's Mom

You will keep in perfect peace
those whose minds are steadfast,
because they trust in you.

—ISAIAH 26:3

Kathi

Roger and I had been married for about three months when his ex-wife e-mailed him to figure out plans for Christmas. When Roger told me this, I thought nothing of it. Of course she wanted to know when she was having the kids and when we would. But that wasn't exactly the tone of the e-mail. No, she wanted to know when she, Roger, and their kids would be having *their* annual holiday celebration.

We are more in step now, but this definitely was a rough way to start off our first holiday.

As I talk to more and more stepmoms, I'm beginning to realize that each blended family has some crazy story just like this when it comes to the relationship with our husbands' ex-wives. Weird expectations, bad patterns, and guilt-motivated compromises are just some of the issues we need to navigate when it comes to making room for the ex.

That's one of the first lessons I learned: As hard as it is, as much as you want to resist doing it, you have to make room for his ex in your blended family. And let me say something else right along with that: It does get easier (much easier!) for you and for her.

This looks entirely different for every situation. Some stepmoms and exes become good friends, or just have the drive and temperaments to make the relationship work. Others cannot and will not be in the same room together. Most of us have a relationship that falls somewhere in between.

We come into the situation at a disadvantage. It's already a bad scene: The mom and dad (your husband) are not on the same page. And once you're in the picture, those feelings don't magically go away. In fact, there are a lot of reasons his ex may not be your biggest fan—a few you have some control over, but most you don't. Here are eight reasons his ex and you may be at a disadvantage:

1. *You remind her of a failing in her life.* However you look at it, no one puts "divorced" at the top of a résumé. Divorce is a failing that can carry a lot of guilt not just for years but for decades. In Roger's case, that meant for many years, Roger, his kids, and his ex were able to celebrate holidays and birthdays together, do family activities together, and even go on vacation together. Roger and his ex thought they were doing what was best for the kids. But that can be confusing not only for the kids but for the parents after a divorce. So when I came on the scene, Roger's kids, as well as Roger, had to forge a new kind of relationship with their mom. I know that as the "new wife," I am a constant reminder to Roger's ex that things didn't work out in their marriage, and that can be painful. Sometimes it's not about you; it's about the circumstances.

2. *You threaten her relationship with her kids.* Almost no one goes into this parenting game thinking some other woman will help raise her children. It's got to be an awful feeling to think that a woman who

was picked by the man you divorced gets to have an impact on your kids.

A few years ago, as Roger and I were taking our girls to Disneyland, I posted on Facebook, "Roger and I are taking our daughters to D-Land! Woot, woot!"

Not long after, Roger got a text from his ex-wife: "I'm glad that Kathi and Amanda have a good relationship, but could you ask her not to call Amanda her 'daughter'? I am her mother, not her."

My first reaction was "Oh, brother." (I mentioned that mercy is not high on my list of gifts.) But even though I felt she was overreacting, I didn't want to step on toes. I'm careful how I post things on Facebook now. I may not always get it right, but having to watch my words on Facebook is a small price to pay for having peace with Roger's ex.

I also make sure that I reinforce to my stepkids that I know their mom is their mom, and I'm not trying to take anyone's place. When they were teens, I would casually ask if they remembered that Mother's Day was coming up and see if they were planning anything. (My husband would do this as well, for both his ex-wife and for me.) In the first several years of our marriage, I would insist that I didn't need for his kids to do anything for me, so they would always celebrate with their mom. But over the past several years, his kids have always recognized me on Mother's Day (which is lovely, but something I didn't dare hope for). As stepmoms, we can go a long way in establishing trust with our stepkids by always being respectful and encouraging of their mom.

Often, when the kids may be annoyed by their own mom, I'm able to come alongside and give a "mom's-eye view" of the situation: "She's just concerned about your safety. You can understand that, right?" or "As a mom, I would want to know who you're hanging out with as well."

3. *You enjoy some of the "perks" she no longer has.* You and your husband are married; his ex may not be. Your husband now has someone

to help with school pickups and dropoffs and figure out how to feed the troops, and maybe you now are a two-income family. Sometimes it's hard when an ex sees the things she used to be able to afford, and now some other woman is enjoying them. It may be easier for you and your husband to give his kids some of the necessities (or little luxuries) of life, including vacations, clothes, and lessons. We all want to provide well for our kids, and it may be hard for our husbands' exes to see us doing that.

4. *Your husband is a different guy with you than he was with her.* I've heard this a lot from our friends and his family. Since we married, my husband has felt the freedom to become more of what God designed him to be. (Don't get me wrong. I know I definitely got the better end of this deal.) Something happens when we are known and loved by another person that makes us act as the best version of ourselves.

With all the stress, disappointment, and drama that come at the end of a bad marriage and then a divorce, it's no wonder that an ex-wife might feel she got the worst end of the deal, while you got the new-and-improved version of her fixer-upper.

5. *Your husband has become a better dad since you got married.* Maybe you remind your husband of important milestones in his kid's life, like his seven-and-a-half-year-old's half birthday. So he stops at the store, gets a donut, and gives half to his daughter with half a candle in it.

Yeah, that has "amazing dad" written all over it, doesn't it?

You help your husband get this dad thing right. And his ex resents you for it. "Why couldn't he have been a good dad when we were to-gether? Must be nice to have someone else do all the heavy lifting when it comes to parenting."

While his ex wants the best for her kids—and the best is a dad who loves his kids and is involved—it burns a little extra that you are the one who is helping him step up. It's a natural feeling, and one that's hard to deal with for anyone who was married before.

6. *You're moving in on her territory.* I've heard lots of stories of step-moms taking their stepdaughters to get their ears pierced, shopping for their dresses for junior high graduation, or taking them for their first mani-pedi. For some moms, those things are important firsts, and as stepmoms, we need to be careful how we navigate those important milestones.

Amanda had all of her significant firsts before I came along. Mani-cures, pedicures, graduation dresses—those were all with her mom (or dad), and that's how it needed to be. But in some families, Mom isn't around or isn't an everyday part of her stepkid's life. In those circum-stances, I think we need to do our best to think about what is best for the child and to not put him or her in the middle of any difficult circumstances.

As a mom, there are certain things I would like to have "first dibs" on with my own kids. But I also understand that it's not about me; it's about them. Some of my kids' firsts have been with their dad and step-mom, and that's okay. But I will make it clear that things like shopping for wedding dresses and attending grandbabies' births go to mom and dad first. Yes, they are adults at this point, and they get to choose. But I would defer to my stepchild and his or her mom for those traditional mom-child moments.

7. *You're an unknown factor.* For my own kids, I've done back-ground checks on babysitters, asked their friends' parents sly questions to get a feel for whose house I'm dropping them off at, and checked out the Facebook pages of the friends they are hanging out with. (You may call it stalking; I call it good parenting.)

But now, your husband's ex is being forced to allow him, who may be the most difficult person in her life, to decide whom her kids live with. You're going to have different chore standards, food, bed-time routines, and discipline at your house. You—yes you—are the unknown factor in her kids' lives, and that has got to feel a little disarming. Especially if she is the kind of mom who labeled her kids' underwear with their names and phone numbers and thought that kid GPS systems were a plausible solution to tracking teens.

8. *You hurt their marriage.* Roger and his wife had been divorced for almost a decade when he and I started to date. But if we're going to talk about reasons an ex may resent the stepmom, we have to acknowledge that some of us didn't take the right road when it came to being with our husbands. If you are someone who was with your husband while he was still married to his wife, there is a real reason she may feel resentment toward you. She may blame you (and your husband) for breaking up her marriage. If this is the case, it is unreasonable to expect your husband's ex to "just get over it." There has been a huge breach of trust—for both her and for their kids.

In the movies, all is forgiven because the ones who had an affair really loved each other and were "meant to be together." But when any relationship starts with brokenness, it doesn't just affect the couple, it affects everyone who was a part of that family.

If none of my other calls to get into counseling have gotten you to make an appointment, please let this one do it. There is not only the grief of your stepkids losing their family, they also will see their dad—and you—differently. Get a Christian professional involved. A counselor can help guide you through the steps it will take to seek healing for everyone involved—for example, admitting your role in the breakup, repentance, seeking forgiveness from those who've been hurt. A counselor will offer advice on what your stepkids may need in order to respect and love you and their dad.

OKAY, SHE DOESN'T LIKE ME. NOW WHAT?

So, what do you do when your husband's ex doesn't like you? Perhaps she's even openly hostile toward you, no matter how hard you've tried to be nice—or at least civil. Again, stepstuff like this is difficult, but remember that you always have a choice about how you will respond to unkind or unfair treatment. Here are a few important guidelines to keep in mind as you forge (or try to mend) a relationship with your husband's ex-wife:

- *Accept the relationship where it's at.* However or whenever your relationship with your husband first started, you have to start to rebuild a difficult relationship with his ex from where you are now. You must move forward with the assumption that everyone is hoping for the best for each other and for the kids. (I know, there may be cases where that's not true, but it's a good place to start for most of us.)

- *Figure out how to move forward in the way that's healthiest for everyone.* When Roger and I were going to counseling to figure out the best way to help Jeremy accept the new stepfamily situation, our therapist suggested that we all (Roger, me, and his ex-wife) come in for group counseling. When Roger suggested this to Jeremy's mom, she said, "I'll go, but not if Kathi goes." She said she didn't see why I needed to be there, since I wasn't one of Jeremy's parents. (Even though Jeremy was living at our house full-time at that point.)

    The child inside of me wanted to lash out. I may have even said something supermature to Roger, like, "Well, if she's not going, then why do I have to?"

    Roger was the one who wisely reminded me that we weren't in this parenting thing to "win," or for momentary comforts. We wanted what was best for everyone, and that included Jeremy. And while we couldn't force anyone to go to therapy, we still had a choice about how we behaved.

    So Roger and I went to therapy.

    As stepmoms, our first instincts aren't always our best

instincts. But we can act better than our first instincts. God has given us the Holy Spirit to help us in life. We can wait, pray, seek wise counsel, and behave better than we feel so much of the time.

- *Understand that God has given you everything you need to respond in a grace-filled way.* It's very humbling to be put in the bad-guy role all the time. But we have submitted ourselves to a powerful God who calls us to act better than we can on our own.

- *Treat the relationship like that of junior high girls, until otherwise notified.* I'm not saying that ex-wives and stepmoms act like junior high girls. But I do remember what it was like to try to have a new relationship at that tender age. There were jealousies, a certain amount of weirdness, and other people watching your every move and judging you. What I am saying is that both of you are in this powder keg of a relationship that you didn't have a lot of say in creating, and until you find yourself on better footing, be cautious.

   Roger's ex and I are in a much better place than we were when we started off. I don't gossip behind her back, I only speak well of her in front of her kids, and I do my best to honor her because, well, she is my stepkids' mom and deserves that respect. She is also a person who has been hurt and is growing. I can relate to those two things because they describe me as well.

- *Pray for her on a regular basis.* Roger's ex is one of the most important people in my stepkids' lives. And my stepkids are two of the most important people in my husband's life and mine. I need to be praying for her and the relationship she has with her kids, as well as with me and my husband. The bonus? It's hard to look for the bad in someone you're

praying for on a regular basis. Often, I've looked for specific
Scripture verses to pray for her. That seems like the best way
to pray for someone when maybe—just maybe—your heart
isn't in it at this moment.

BOUNDARIES ARE IMPORTANT

One day I came home to find Roger's ex in our kitchen baking cookies.
To say I was surprised is an understatement. I tried to be as gracious as
possible, but then asked, "How did you get into the house?"

Her response? "Oh, I have a key. I told Roger since my kids live
here, I needed to have a key."

Of course, I had a follow-up conversation with Roger, to which
he replied, "Yeah, I forgot about that. She's always had a key. And the
oven at her place hasn't worked for a while, so she bakes over here."

What? This was new information to me.

"Until now, right?" I smiled in a way that told him I meant business.

"Yes. Until now," Roger replied.

This whole situation may seem like the weirdest thing to you—
Roger's ex-wife having the key to our house and coming over to bake.
But I've come to understand that in most blended families, someone has had to strike some sort of deal to "get along." To not rock
the boat. To just keep everything calm. We all have these weird little
arrangements.

And some of those deals are important to keep. Your husband's
ex sends your stepkids home with piles of laundry, even though that's
not what the custody agreement states. And you decide, "This is not
the hill I'm willing to die on." Good for you. There are times when we
need to make compromises for the sake of peace.

But I really wasn't okay with someone who wasn't one of our kids
having access to all the areas of our home when I wasn't there. So

Roger asked for the key back. And when she kept forgetting to bring it back, we went ahead and had the locks changed. Not because I was concerned that she was going to do anything wrong, but because I wanted peace of mind in my own home.

Shortly afterward, Amanda, my stepdaughter, asked me, "Why don't you like my mom?"

Oh, those words broke my heart.

"Amanda, why do you think I don't like your mom?" I wanted to get to the core issue of her question.

"Because you asked for the key back that she had to the house," she said.

I knew that trying to explain the delicacies of a stepfamily situation was too much. So I took a different route. "Amanda, you have a boyfriend. Imagine that you both went to the same school and shared a locker. Now imagine that his ex-girlfriend also had the combination to that locker. How would that make you feel?"

Now I was speaking a language that Amanda could understand. She said, "I wouldn't like that."

"That's all I'm saying. Look, Amanda, your mom is welcome anytime. I would just like to know when she's going to be here. She will always be invited for birthdays and celebrations for you or your brother. But the keys to our house are just for people who live here."

When You're the Ex

I'm not only a stepmom. A few years ago, my kids' dad got remarried, so now I'm also the ex-wife in another couple's marriage. Isn't this blended-family stuff fun? (Good luck to my kids as they pull together their *Ancestry.com* tree.)

My kids were pretty much of legal age when their dad remarried, so their stepmom was never on the receiving end of homework duties or doing my kids' laundry. But still, she plays an important role in my kids' lives. And if I'm being honest, she does a pretty good job of it.

I've only met her a handful of times, but when my ex remarried, I have to admit I was concerned about the role his new wife would play in my kids' lives. But she has surprised me and has done many things right:

1. *She celebrates with my kids.* Whether it's a graduation, a birthday, or some other milestone, my kids' stepmom is there to cheer them on. She came into their lives when they were already teenagers and living full-time with me and my husband, so she was never responsible for their day-to-day care. But she and my ex included them in their wedding, which was really important to my kids, and she has been there for their celebrations as well.

2. *She loves their dad.* I want my kids to be surrounded by examples of what a healthy marriage looks like. It makes me happy to know that my ex and his wife are providing that for my kids. They post great pictures on Facebook of running together and taking vacations. My kids share the photos with me, and it always makes me happy to know that my kids are seeing how much their dad and his wife love and enjoy each other.

3. *She includes my kids in activities and traditions.* My kids' stepmom was born in a different country and has different traditions from those my kids grew up with. She shares her traditions with them and respects my kids' traditions as well. She loves many of the things my kids love (baseball, Tolkien, *Doctor Who*) and will often include them in trips and games, and always tags them on Facebook.

4. *She encourages my kids to have a relationship with their dad.* My kids see their dad on a pretty regular basis, sometimes

with their stepmom, but most of the time without. I think my kids' time with their dad has actually increased since their marriage. Though I couldn't stay married to their dad, I always wanted to make sure my kids have a relationship with him. She encourages that.

5. *She takes her cues from my kids.* Does that mean she lets my kids lead? No. But she has also never forced them to call her Mom. She spent as much time with them as they were comfortable with at first; and she has been there when they've needed her.

6. *I've never heard a negative word from her about our family.* This is a big deal, since I know how negative words can hurt families. But she has been stellar at saying nothing negative.

I asked both my kids if they were comfortable with me writing about their stepmom. My daughter's response? "It used to make me sad that you and Dad weren't together, but now that I have Roger and Maita in my life, I feel really lucky. Neither of them tries to be my parent, but I know they are on my side."

And isn't that what we want—for our kids and stepkids to have a bunch of adults on their side, cheering them on?

EIGHT

Say This, Not That

The tongue has the power of life and death.

—Proverbs 18:21

Carol

I love the scene in Western movies where a craggy-faced outlaw crawls up the side of a cliff carrying a box of nitroglycerin to blow up a railroad track. The fear in his eyes captures me. The whistle blows as the train approaches. My stomach churns. I jump at every rock that crumbles beneath his hand, which quivers as he struggles on the ledge. The box of nitro dangles, ready to explode at his first stumble.

I'm a wreck, anticipating the explosion. Actually, you and I live out this scenario every day.

That nitro? Our words. God says that our tongues possess "the power of life and death" (Proverbs 18:21). Our words can wound ourselves and others. And with one misstep, we can blow relationships to kingdom come. I know because I've done it. You, too? I'm ashamed of how often I have used my words as weapons. I have put my foot in my mouth so often that at times I couldn't even hobble, much less walk.

When it comes to using our words in blended-family situations, we need to be especially sensitive. There came a point when I knew I needed help, so I studied what God says about words and how to use them. Thankfully He gives clear guidelines in His Word. Later in the chapter, I share specific words you can use to build and strengthen relationships within your stepfamily. Words are that important and that powerful. Let's take a look at how Scripture covers this important topic:

> If anyone considers himself religious and yet does not keep a tight rein on his tongue, he deceives himself and his religion is worthless. (James 1:26)

> With the tongue we praise our Lord and Father, and with it we curse men, who have been made in God's likeness. Out of the same mouth come praise and cursing. My brothers, this should not be. (James 3:9–10)

> Reckless words pierce like a sword,
>> but the tongue of the wise brings healing.
>>> (Proverbs 12:18)

> Do you see a man who speaks in haste?
>> There is more hope for a fool than for him.
>>> (Proverbs 29:20)

> Therefore each of you must put off falsehood and speak truthfully to his neighbor, for we are all members of one body. (Ephesians 4:25)

> Do not let any unwholesome talk come out of your mouths, but only what is helpful for building others up according to their needs, that it may benefit those who listen. (Ephesians 4:29)

> All kinds of animals, birds, reptiles and creatures of the sea are being tamed and have been tamed by man, but no man can tame the tongue. (James 3:7–8)

These and other verses tell us that words are important to God. And that last verse from James, as well as my own experience, shows me that I need God's help to choose words that encourage, uplift, inspire, and motivate, especially when I don't feel like it. I have blown it often, and my guess is that you have too.

But there's good news for people like us! The right words can help rebuild what the wrong words have blown apart. We'll look at rebuilding words a little more in the forgiveness chapter. But first let's lay a firm foundation so we don't stumble as often when it comes to how we speak to the people around us. In addition to asking God to help you be wise with your words, consider the following:

- Ask God to give you a *realistic* vision of yourself as the kind of stepmother you want to be (and He wants you to be), including how you want to act and the words you want to speak—those things *you* can control. Keep this vision in mind and ask God to help bring it about.
- Picture ahead of time *how you want to respond* to your stepchildren (and your biological children)—what you want to do and say—in line with your predetermined vision. Your thoughts are powerful. They will set the stage.
- Set yourself up for success by preparing, even role-playing, and practicing your words and tone. Now you are good to go.

SAY THIS, NOT THAT

Stepmoms need a ready reference for those inevitable moments that catch us off guard. Don't take the bait of comments intended to antagonize or hurt you. You'll be hooked like a large-mouth bass out of a crystal-clear lake, floundering and flip-flopping and gasping for breath. I repeat: Do not take the bait. Your stepkids may or may not act out of deliberate meanness. It may be their immaturity and insecurity talking. Either way, respond with calm authority in your words and actions. And memorize this handy chart:

What They Say/Do	What You Say/Do	Not This!
"You're not my real mom!"	"You're right."	"Praise God!"
"I don't have to listen to you!"	"The rule is . . ."	"Oh yes, you do!"
"I hate you!"	"We'll talk later." Then leave the scene.	"Back at ya!"
"You're a witch!" (or a similar rhyming word)	Say nothing. Leave the scene.	"Takes one to know one."
"You're so mean!"	"I'm not trying to be mean. I'm sorry it feels that way to you."	"You don't know how good you have it!"

Following are a few more important tips to remember when it comes to how we use our words:

- Remember, even if your stepchild is an adult, or even if your stepchild is older than you, lead by example. Model desired behavior. Never name-call, swear, or scream, even if your stepkids do. This honors them *and* you and goes a long way toward relationship building. Gary and Greg Smalley write in *Bound by Honor* that you can give honor to others "regardless of whether or not they 'deserve' it, because, like love, it's an act of the will."[1] Why is this so important? "Our experience and our research indicate that increasing honor and decreasing anger in the home are the two main principles in raising healthy teenagers."[2] It also works well with adults and stepchildren of all ages.

- It's never a good time to make your point to a stepchild or deal with an underlying issue in the heat of anger. Wait until cooler minds prevail. Counting to ten is a good idea.
- When you're verbally attacked, Christian therapist and stepmom Deborah Tyrrell suggests listening for and validating feelings. When a stepchild screams, "I hate you!" how can you respond to it doesn't fuel the fire? Here are three possibilities:
  1. "You're angry."
  2. "You hate how you're feeling now."
  3. "I understand you're upset."
- Tyrrell advises to invite input, listen, and be a safe person with whom your stepchildren can share their feelings. It takes a stepmom secure in herself to do this, however. As Beth Moore writes in *So Long, Insecurity*, "If you think insecurity makes run-of-the-mill parenting difficult, it can make the challenges of stepparenting nearly debilitating."[3] Tyrrell counsels stepmoms to remind themselves, *I am okay whether this child likes me or not. It's not really about me.*
- Tyrrell also suggests apologizing for your offenses, which goes a long way toward mending relationships. You can still see yourself as valuable even though you are fallible, she adds.
- In *Parenting Today's Adolescent*, Dennis and Barbara Rainey write, "The time to address anger in a child is *not* in the midst of an argument or heated words. You may need to give your teenager some time to cool off or to remind him to choose his words carefully. . . . A child who is full of anger and expressing it wrongly is like a mud wrestler. A parent must stay outside the ring, remaining as objective and loving as possible. When a parent joins the child in slinging mud emotionally and irrationally, he has stepped into the mud puddle and become a mud wrestler too."[4]

- Sometimes the written word is the best answer. You can write things that may be harder to say face-to-face. A note can be reread. A note can be kept. However, a note can also be shown to others or shared on Facebook. So a word of caution: Be sure anything you write is something you wouldn't mind being read to the world.
- Never shout, "Shut up!" at your stepchild. Besides being rude, it's dangerous. Kids hear it as, "I don't want to hear you," and therefore, "You and what you say don't matter to me." Also, anything you say can be repeated to someone else, resulting in unintended consequences that can backfire on you, including but not limited to an ex seeking sole custody. Consider this as one of your Miranda rights as a stepmom: "Anything you say can and will be used against you."

And speaking of words *not* to say, if stepchildren report back to you any unkind things their biological mother may have said about you, it's wise not to respond in kind. In fact, you don't have to respond at all. First of all, you can't control what someone says about you; you can only control your response. And if you weren't there, you don't know what was actually said. Second, you do not have to defend yourself. You can say something like, "I'm sorry she thinks that." Even if it takes every ounce of self-control you possess, you will never regret staying silent on this one. If you have to, just walk away. Stepchildren will see you respond with grace while under fire, and they'll trust your words as you teach them to do the same, which is also known as "practicing what you preach." Well done, stepmom.

It's also wise not to discuss one child's issues with other children in the family. Things have a way of getting misinterpreted and misunderstood. And things said in confidence can be repeated in a moment of carelessness, destroying any trust you may have begun to build up.

Similarly, do not discuss with the children any issues you have with their father. That's adult business.

PROPER PRAISE

A modern-day truism says, "It is easier to train up a child than it is to repair an adult. Choose your words wisely." Praise is one way to use words to build relationships. We all like to hear nice things about ourselves. Psychologists have discovered that praise is more effective, however, when it acknowledges something that required effort, not for a common achievement (breathing in and breathing out, for example) or just for something to say. Kids can tell the difference. They will tune out constant praise as meaningless and insincere. While building or strengthening the connection with your stepchildren, try the following tips, making them age appropriate:

- *Praise the effort, even if the desired result isn't achieved.* "You showed courage when you tried out for the team, ran for class president, asked for that raise," and so on.
- *Praise originality.* "Not every cat has blue fur. Yours looks distinctive in this painting" sounds more encouraging than "A cat with blue fur? That's ridiculous."
- *Praise behavior as well as beauty.* We praise what we value. While we want our stepchildren to know we think they're attractive, we want them to know we value their character even more highly. Physical beauty can fade. Character can grow more beautiful with time. For example: "I like how you gave up your seat for that older gentleman. That was a thoughtful and kind thing to do." And while we're talking about beauty, avoid commenting on what you perceive as a flaw. Don't say, "You're not really going to have a second

piece of cake, are you?" and never comment on their bud-
ding or blatant sexuality. "You look hot in those jeans" is
better left unsaid. Phrase your comments in such a way that
they are age appropriate and sensitive.

- *Praise character, labeling the trait and how you respond to it.*
  Don't just say, "Good girl!" as you would to a pet. Rather, say,
  "You showed respect when you cleared the dishes as I asked.
  I appreciate that." Don't label the person, however. If you say,
  "You're kind," your stepchild may respond, "No, I'm not,"
  and then you've started an argument that nobody can win.

- *Praise in simple words.* Try "I love to watch you dance, swim,
  play basketball . . ." or some other activity they enjoy. Or "I
  love to listen to you sing, play piano, talk so nicely . . ." No
  need to elaborate. Avoid saying, "But next time try . . ." Let
  your stepchildren know you enjoy them, or at least something they do.

One of my favorite verses is Ephesians 4:32: "Be kind and compassionate to one another, forgiving each other, just as in Christ God
forgave you." Being kind includes choosing to speak to people better
than they deserve. This is how God speaks to us. It includes taking the
initiative to speak words that heal, encourage, and inspire.

Our first summer as a blended family, I looked for ways Abby
and I could have fun doing "sweet surprises" for others. We looked up
Bible verses on the importance of loving people, and over McDonald's
Happy Meals, we made a list of ways we could do that. We talked about
how good it would feel to know we had obeyed God, and how much
fun we would have showing others how special they were to us. I told
Abby that people enjoyed it when she treated them with kindness, the
same way she liked it when people treated her that way. I assured her
she would be great at doing things that make others feel special.

Abby took it all in.

She thought of ideas, and I wrote them down: Bake cookies for Dad. Take some flowers to Granny and Grandpa Boley. Sing a song for Granny Jane and Grandpa Dan. Make a card for Grandpa Joe and Grandma Flo.

"What could we do for your aunts and uncles?" I asked.

"Draw a picture?" she suggested.

"Great idea!" I said. "I like how you're thinking of lots of ways to be kind."

Abby looked at me and smiled. "I just want to show love," she said. Bingo! Proper praise can help you lead your children and stepchildren exactly where you want them to go.

Giving supportive feedback and positive reinforcement makes kids "want to keep doing what they're doing,"[5] according to Dr. Thomas K. Connellan in his book *Bringing Out the Best in Others*.

Here's the formula. Positive reinforcement requires that first you "catch 'em doing good" and then:

- Reinforce positive behavior immediately.
- Reinforce *any* improvement, not just excellence.
- Reinforce positive behavior specifically.
- Reinforce new behavior continually.
- Reinforce good habits intermittently.[6]

Every now and then, let your children and stepchildren overhear you saying positive things about them to their father or stepfather. Stage it, if necessary. Those words carry extra weight.

AFFIRMING WORDS

Use *affirming words* to express your understanding, support, and belief in your stepkids. Even into their early teens, kids tend to believe what adults tell them about themselves. Say these phrases, or ones that fit your situation, regularly, at the most appropriate times. You speak confidence and hope, "a positive expectation of good," into your step-kids' lives when you say the following:

- You're making wiser decisions.
- Your smile lights up the room.
- You're becoming more organized.
- You're quicker to obey.
- You're becoming more thoughtful.

Not seeing anything yet to affirm? Then give them something to shoot for. You can speak what you hope to see in the future:

- You're going to do great things for God someday.
- You'll make a good parent one day.
- You will inspire others.
- You will figure this out.

If it seems awkward at first, go ahead and plow right through. We've already accepted that awkward is part of our reality as stepmoms. We can handle awkward. And remember: God says your words have "the power of life and death" (Proverbs 18:21). We get to choose, and awkward seems a small price to pay for speaking life into our stepkids' lives.

PUT WORDS TO WORK FOR YOU

The words we choose as we interact with our stepkids can *help prevent* behavior meltdowns and contribute to cooperation. But there's more to words than just the words themselves. Tone and volume make all the difference. So do body language and facial expression.

Check out the following tips to help you hit just the right note when it's necessary to give direction:

- *Tone it down.* The louder you yell, the more kids tune you out. They miss the message, usually only picking up your anger. And that can give them a sense of power and control over you. *Look what I can make her do!* they think. They have pushed your buttons, and they have won, in their eyes. But we know better. No one wins when you yell. Use a kind and firm tone.

- *Be specific.* Say, "Your shoes go in your bedroom," not, "I would like it if you put your shoes away." Your stepkids may not care what you would like and may test you to see what you will do. If they need reminding, say, "The rule is . . ." or if it carries more weight, say, "Your father said the rule is . . ."
- *Be decisive.* Pastor and stepdad Chip Ingram writes in *Effective Parenting in a Defective World,* "I believe about 80 percent of your need to discipline will be eliminated if you learn to say what you mean and mean what you say. Children are much less likely to pester a parent with repeated requests if the parent is decisive."[7]
- *Mean what you say the first time.* If you mean what you say only when you reach the boiling point, kids learn they can ignore you until then. Don't let them wear you down. Be strong, stepmom!
- *But if they do keep pestering?* A reply borrowed from the courtroom works well: "Asked and answered." Said with a smile.
- *Never add "Okay?" at the end of a direction.* That leaves it open for kids to say no, which is not okay. You aren't asking for their opinion or permission. You are making a statement.
- *Be clear and concise.* Give directions in as few words as possible. "The trash goes outside." Don't get into a drawn-out explanation or debate. Clear and concise, that's you.

Words for His Ears Alone

Your husband needs your words of comfort, support, and admiration. Life in a stepfamily is tough for him, too. He needs to know you understand and respect him for who he is and what he does for your family.

See Kathi's book *The Husband Project*[8] for additional—and fun—ways to express your appreciation. Also remember, as enjoyable and interesting as it is to discuss sports, politics, and religion with your husband, don't forget the romance. You are the only woman with whom he can flirt and have a sexy conversation. And if it leads to more? Well, you're also the only woman with whom he can have sex. Enough said.

Wisdom for Savvy Stepmoms in Ten Words or Less

Wisdom is a precious commodity for stepmoms as we grapple with the challenges, joys, and pitfalls of blended-family life. In the midst of the struggle, we can easily forget our priorities, lose perspective, and start to believe things that just aren't so. In moments of frustration or fatigue, we may succumb to the temptation to lash out in our words or actions. We may become discouraged when our stepkids or our husbands' exes criticize us or hurl flaming arrows our way. We may feel as if we're dealing with this stepstuff alone, and no one else truly understands what we're going through.

Whatever your situation, stepmom, a little wisdom along the way can be invaluable in restoring your perspective and regrounding you in the truth. Put these ten little nuggets of wisdom, supplied in reverse order, into practice and keep them handy whenever you need some helpful reminders:

10 annoying words stepmoms hear: "But they're just children. They only want to be loved." This is simply not true. You know it and take comfort in the fact that other stepmoms know it too. True, everybody needs, and most people want, to be loved. But sometimes "they" are teenagers; sometimes they are adults. And sometimes they want to destroy your marriage. Take what some people say with a grain of salt. It may be well-intentioned, but you know better.

9 words never to speak again: "You always . . . You never . . . You should . . . Why did you . . . ?" These are phrases to strike from your vocabulary. Nobody likes to be falsely accused ("always" and "never" are rarely true) or told what to do. And "Why did you . . ?" almost always implies the silent answer "Because I'm a dummy." You can build your stepchildren's respect for you and trust in you by avoiding these nine little words.

8 words that can build goodwill: "I am so blessed to be your stepmother." I know. You may not feel it or think it all the time. But when you start to believe it by faith, watch what happens to your attitude and your actions. You'll start to see blessings you didn't see before. You'll start to think about things differently. You'll begin to feel more peaceful. And you can't help but radiate "good vibes" to your kids and stepkids (and even your husband's ex).

7 words that instantly increase your joy: "Celebrate everything. There are no small victories." You will have more fun this way and enjoy your life more. And when you start to look for the victories, you'll find more of them to celebrate. Celebrate even the smallest things: You held your tongue when you wanted to explode; you complimented every child at least once today, even if it was for something as simple as an appropriate color choice in clothing; you resisted that second scoop of fudge-brownie ice cream. Celebrate! Just be sure to rejoice in healthy ways. While you are celebrating, beware of overspending or overindulging in any way.

6 words that can save your life as well as your reputation: "When in doubt, shut your mouth." You will save yourself heartache and embarrassment if you follow this wise advice. One of the worst things you can say is, "You just need to . . ." That isn't helpful. You don't always have to prove you are right. You don't always have to correct people. You don't always have to have the last word. You don't always have to say what you think or how you feel. Joshua and the Israelites marched around the walled city of Jericho once each day for six days under orders from God not to give a war cry or raise their voices or say a word. On the seventh day, they marched six times in silence around the city, and then the seventh time around, Joshua commanded them to shout. That's when the walls came tumblin' down. One of the biggest lessons I learned from reading about Joshua and the battle of Jericho was that sometimes the best way to win a battle is to know when to keep your mouth shut.

5 words that will save your sanity: "What does the Word say?" The Bible is always our go-to guide. But it takes more than acknowledging what the Word says. We must act on what we learn. We can change our thinking to agree with God's thoughts. When we do that, we renew our minds and find ourselves more peaceful, more content, wiser, and more joyful. Just like the demon-possessed man, we are only in our right minds when we sit at the feet of Jesus (Mark 5:15). The Bible is God's love letter to us. Reading part of it each morning helps set our hearts and minds for the day, but if you're sharper in the evening, do it then, or whenever works best for you. Schedule it in. It's that important.

4 words that will improve your life: "Take care of yourself." You're important, stepmom. You're valuable. You're loved. You're worth taking care of. In addition, if you don't take care of yourself physically, mentally, spiritually, and emotionally, you can't take care of others. We all need to eat healthy food, drink plenty of water, and get enough exercise and restful sleep. Claim some "me" time. Connect with close friends with whom you can share your heart. Laugh. Would you benefit from some counseling?

You are worth every penny. Above all, nourish your spirit by enjoying your relationship with Jesus. Speaking about our needs, Drs. Henry Cloud and John Townsend write in *12 "Christian" Beliefs That Can Drive You Crazy*, "Neglecting them leads to spiritual and emotional problems; having them met, however, frees us to meet the needs of others cheerfully and without resentment."[9] It's not selfish to make self-care a priority. It's essential.

3 words that will increase your influence with your stepkids: "Never criticize anyone." As we said earlier, never criticize your stepkids' biological mom, even if she is serving time in the state pen as an ax murderer. Seriously. Children hold deep loyalty for their biological parents, even if they desert them, neglect them, or mistreat them. Criticizing a parent sounds as if you're criticizing the child. Besides, criticizing others makes you look small and can open the door for unnecessary conflict.

2 words that will keep you from worry: "Pray continually." Stay connected. As you get to know Jesus better, you'll find more of your prayers reflecting thanks for what He has done, is doing, and will do, according to His promises. This is balm for your heart and fills you with peace. You will notice you don't worry so much. You'll feel calmer and act more stable. You can benefit from connecting with others of similar faith as well. Their support is invaluable. Find a Bible-believing church where you can worship on a regular basis. If you've ever wondered what God's will is for your life, prayer is part of it (1 Thessalonians 5:17).

1 word that makes this whole thing possible: "Believe." You can do this, stepmom. We believe in you.

One more thing that can help stepmoms: laughter. One day I felt angry, sad, and depressed. Not wanting to stay that way, I went to my bookcase and pulled out a scrapbook I started in college of cartoons, cards, and clippings that always make me laugh. There in one column were the cows standing upright on their hind legs, drinking coffee from mugs and laughing. In the next column, they were down on all fours again chewing cud after one of them yelled the warning, "Car!" as a convertible sped by. It makes me laugh even now, just remembering. I emerged from my room with such a changed countenance that my family wanted to know what had happened. "I just spent thirty minutes with my scrapbook," I answered.

I also keep handy DVDs of movies and television shows that I find

Seven Things Super-Stepmoms Say Often

1. Please.
2. Thank you.
3. You're welcome.
4. I forgive you (when appropriate and not in a holier-than-thou tone). As my husband says, "Rush to grace." Don't just mutter "Uh-huh" when people say they are sorry or ask forgiveness. It's important—and healing—for people to hear these words.
5. I'm sorry. Say it as often as necessary. (For some of us, it's necessary more often than for others.) Never, however, apologize for sticking to your word or backing up your husband's rules (and eventually your husband's and your rules). It's good to say, "I'm sorry I lost my temper." It's confusing if you say, "I'm sorry I made you pick up your shoes," even if you acted in anger.
6. What do you think? Ask your stepkids for their opinions and really listen.
7. I appreciate how you . . . Fill in the blank with something your stepkids do that you appreciate.

hilarious. And if life in a stepfamily doesn't provide you with enough material for a good belly laugh, try keeping a few books on hand just for that purpose. Personally, anything by Erma Bombeck or Dave Barry never fails to crack me up.

Remember to laugh. Keep a sense of humor. Laughing relieves tension and increases the endorphins your brain releases. Scientific studies show that laughter can improve your immune system, relieve pain, make it easier to cope with difficult situations, and—very important for stepmoms—help you connect with other people. Sounds like something God told us a long time ago: "A cheerful heart is good medicine, but a crushed spirit dries up the bones" (Proverbs 17:22).

I also started writing down funny things that our girls said and did or that happened to us as a family. Those journals are now some of my favorites and help us remember good times together. (This especially comes in handy if you're having a hard time remembering if you've *ever* had any good times together.) As a stepfamily, you are building your own unique set of memories. Like the time we let each of the girls pick a CD to play in the car on a long road trip, with the qualification that it had to be something we would all enjoy. This was before the days of iPods. Abby chose well. Allison chose well. We complimented them and sang along.

When it was five-year-old Andrea's turn, we thought we would hear Psalty the Singing Songbook or *Kids Sing Bible Songs*, but, boy, were we surprised. When her CD started playing, nobody said a word for several minutes. Then we couldn't hold it in any longer. We all burst out laughing at her choice: a "nature sounds" recording of humpback whales "singing." I'm afraid it hurt her feelings at the time, but now it's a fun memory. And it still cracks us up.

Here's what others have said about laughter:
- "I honestly think it's the thing I like most, to laugh. It cures a multitude of ills." (Audrey Hepburn)

- "If we couldn't laugh we would all go insane." (Robert Frost)
- "I don't trust anyone who doesn't laugh." (Maya Angelou)
- "There is nothing in the world so irresistibly contagious as laughter and good humor." (Charles Dickens)
- "Laughter is carbonated holiness." (Anne Lamott)
- "She can laugh at the days to come." (Proverbs 31:25)

Keep laughing, my friend.

Ten Things Smart Stepmoms Say to Themselves Out Loud Every Day

Not only do we talk to others; we also talk to ourselves all day long. Every day. So let's make the things we say to ourselves something worth hearing. Here are ten powerful, life-giving statements that smart stepmoms repeat to themselves every day:

1. Jesus loves me personally. (John 15:9)
2. I am never alone. (Hebrews 13:5)
3. I am forgiven. (Hebrews 8:12)
4. I am accepted. (Romans 15:7)
5. I am slow to get angry at people and circumstances. (James 1:19)
6. I am quick to forgive. (Ephesians 4:32)
7. I am empowered to do hard things. (Philippians 4:13)
8. I can choose words that give life. (Proverbs 15:4)
9. I can choose my thoughts. (Philippians 4:8)
10. My dignity comes from God and does not depend on what others say about me or how they treat me. (Psalm 62:7)

Why say these things out loud? Won't you feel like an idiot? Maybe at first. But don't let feeling self-conscious keep you from this practice. Nobody will come haul you away, especially if you do it in private. In Hebrew, to *meditate* actually means to "mutter." It's not enough to just think the thoughts; you need to say the words loud enough for your own ears to hear them. The spoken word packs power. Speaking these words helps cement them in our minds.

And don't stop after a day or two. Experts say it takes approximately a month for something to become a habit. Commit to thirty days and then see how you feel. It's like boot camp. It takes awhile to see results. We're training ourselves to think and speak correctly, because how we think and what we believe determines our behavior. And as one of my friends says about talking to herself, "Sometimes it's the only way I can have an intelligent conversation around here!"

ONE HANDY PHRASE TO THE RESCUE

When a situation with your children or stepchildren presents itself and is so stunning it threatens to suck the breath right out of you, you need a go-to phrase that does two things: It lets you respond in a way that keeps the situation from escalating and reminds you to calm down. (Don't ask me how I know this! Let's just say I've lived it.) An older, wiser friend of mine, who as a fellow student helped Billy Graham learn Greek at Wheaton College (one of my alma maters—"Roll Thunder!"), taught me her favorite expression to say to herself in such a situation: "Don't panic. Stay focused." While you're reminding yourself to stay calm and focused, choose a phrase you can speak out loud. Keep it short. Keep it simple. It will buy you time to think of a further response. Consider one of the following:

- "No problem." Even if it's a *huge* problem, it can be best handled when you are calm. "No problem" cues you to take a deep breath and relax before plunging in. And you aren't lying. What you're really saying is, "There's *no problem* here that we can't handle together." You're just taking a shortcut.
- "Okay." It's the one-word equivalent of "I hear you," but it comes across better at the beginning of a conversation. "I

hear you" is a good phrase for later in the conversation, to verify you understand what is being said, which you may not at first, which is why you start out with "Okay."

- "Tell me more." This acknowledges there is *plenty* more and allows you to listen before speaking—always a good choice.
- Choose a word or phrase that you feel comfortable using and can remember in the heat of the moment.

Any of these is better than, *"What the %#$*% did you just say?"* Words start as thoughts. Be careful what thoughts you allow to linger.

I remember one day reliving in my mind the details of every insult, every perceived slight, every veiled criticism that I had ever received. I don't know why. I thought of the perfect comeback for each one, delivered with the full force of a knockout punch. *I'll show them*, I thought, and mentally I went for their jugular. I was good, too. Mentally I brought each person to their knees.

Soon I was so wound up, I was ready to fight over conversations that had never happened anywhere but inside my head. I felt angry, hurt, hostile, and ugly. What would possess me to do such a thing? Nothing good, I can promise you. That's when I learned that if I didn't take control of my thoughts, I would make myself sick and ruin my day *and* that of everyone else I came into contact with. That wasn't how I wanted to live.

I learned that I have to treat my mind as if it's a two-year-old, putting my hands on either side of its face, looking directly into its eyes, and telling it, "We're not going to think about that. We're going to think about this instead," and then substituting a positive thought for the critical, negative, judgmental one (the kind that comes so naturally). As the apostle Paul wrote in Philippians 4:8, "Whatever is true, whatever is noble, whatever is right, whatever is pure, whatever is lovely, whatever is admirable—if anything is excellent or praiseworthy—think about such things." Actually, that's a lovely description of Jesus.

Sometimes we trick ourselves into believing that our thoughts are our own business and nobody else's. Apparently God thinks our thoughts are *His* business. I'm thankful He tells us specific things to think about.

"The words you speak are electromagnetic life forces that come from thoughts inside your brain. They are influenced by your five senses and result from choices you have made. They reflect your attitude,"[10] writes neuroscientist Dr. Caroline Leaf in *Who Switched Off My Brain? Controlling Toxic Thoughts and Emotions.*

She goes on to say,

> Like poison ivy, words have their sting. You may think you'll feel better when you've let it all out and given others a "piece of your mind," but you actually won't. The science of thought and the Word of God are very clear that nothing good comes out of negative words. Negative words can be more harmful to you than the person you say them to, because your mind formed the toxic thought, meditated on the words and spoke them—reinforcing them in your mind. Because you created the negative stronghold, your body reacts with stress. If the stress chemicals flow in your brain for longer than 30 seconds, your thinking, intelligence, body and everything else are all going to be negatively affected.[11]

Wow! Besides showing grace, speaking positive words contributes to my personal health as well as the health of my relationships. And here's a chilling thought: Out-of-control words can lead to out-of-control acts.

So, dear stepmoms, guard your thoughts with due diligence. Ask God to help your thoughts as well as your words honor Him and encourage others. He will always answer yes to that prayer.

It's comforting to remember the Holy Spirit lives in us, and He produces the good fruit within us. It isn't a result of our self-discipline and hard work. Notice the order of the fruit of the Spirit in Galatians 5:22–23: "The fruit of the Spirit is love, joy, peace, patience, kindness, goodness, faithfulness, gentleness and self-control." In a blended family, the evidence of the Spirit's fruit in our lives often emerges in reverse order, beginning with self-control, especially in our words, and leading us toward joy and love.

It's so tempting to think we have no choice but to give in to critical, negative thinking and speaking and to just assume we can't help it. But I can't tell you how many times I've found that if I take just a moment to remind myself that I have *self-control* whether I feel it or not—because God's Spirit lives in me and He produces it—I *actually can control myself.* This is a thrilling discovery! You may be much further along in this area than I am, but I want others who struggle with me to know there is hope.

Don't give up on your journey to love. Don't be discouraged if every step takes longer than you expected. Remember, it takes awhile for fruit to bloom. It takes standard apple trees between six and ten years to produce fruit.

Hang in there, stepmom. You are about to bloom.

Treat and talk to your stepkids the way *you* would want a stepmother to treat and talk to you. Treat them and talk to them the way you would want a stepmother to treat and talk to *your* children. "So in everything, do to others what you would have them do to you" (Matthew 7:12). Jesus thinks this is a good idea, and He'll give you the strength and grace to do it.

NINE

At All Costs, Protect Your Marriage

The wise woman builds her house, but with her

own hands the foolish one tears hers down.

—PROVERBS 14:1

Kathi

Every piece of advice I read as I started my blended family seemed to say the same thing: Make your marriage the priority. You've probably had the same thought I've had: *I bet that was written by some psychologist in a perfect marriage with one seven-year-old daughter who loves staying at Grandma's. How on earth can I make my marriage a priority when I'm just trying to keep from drowning around here?*

In the real world of stepparenting, marriage often comes in fifth place—after kids, stepkids, ex-spouse feuds, and mere survival. And the thought of having a marriage-centered household is about as likely as one of your stepkids choosing you for his or her "The Person I Most Admire" report in junior high.

I know it's hard, but I have to be the one to tell you: The cold, hard truth is that if any of us in blended families want to do more than just eke out an existence and hold on tight until the last kid leaves the house, we must make our marriages a priority, not an afterthought. In fact, I want an awesome marriage. I want to spend a lot of time and a lot of energy loving on this man (and getting loved back).

To go even further, I would be so bold as to say that it's even more important for us as blended families to be laser focused on having an awesome marriage than it is for more traditional families. Why?

• Blended families are thrown into hostile situations.
• There are other parents who get a say in your household.
• Your kids are thrown off balance because of so many life changes.

The benefits to having a marriage-centered blended family are numerous.

1. *It offers a united front when it comes to the kids.* Parenting in a traditional family has enough challenges, but blend in another parent, and it can be downright overwhelming at times. When we put our spouses' needs before our kids' needs, it shows our kids and stepkids that they are not in a divide-and-conquer situation. It gives our kids a sense of security to know that the rules and relationships are not ever changing.

2. *It ensures a united front when it comes to the other parent.* There are going to be battles with the other parent. And when your kids see you working together to solve those problems, they will not only see adults acting like adults (imagine that), but they will also learn that they can't manipulate the situation.

3. *It provides a great example of a healthy marriage for your kids and stepkids.* When my daughter Kim was sixteen, she and I were having a conversation about the boy she was seeing and some of the character issues I was noticing. Though he was a nice guy, he and Kimberly together were not a good match. I told her plainly that I was praying for a relationship like the one Roger and I had. She shocked me by saying, "That's the last thing I want. Roger will do whatever you tell him to do. I want a strong man."

Whoa! Wait a second. That statement cut me to the bone, and I held our conversation as a point of prayer for years. Roger definitely has a more "mellow" personality than I do. And we have had more than our share of disagreements. I tend to shoot from the hip, whereas Roger thoughtfully considers things for a while. While Roger uses facts and figures, historical data, and research, I usually just bring passion and a loud voice to the table. (We balance each other well.)

A few years later, I brought the issue up to Kim again. She said, "Yeah, I was wrong. Roger isn't whipped. You guys just love each other a lot and think of the other person before you think of yourself." It took Kimberly a few years and a few more examples of how semihealthy adults communicate as they try to work out their problems, but eventually she got it. You see, serving each other and listening to the other's opinion aren't usually modeled in the world or on TV. Kim needed help seeing what a healthy marriage really looks like (and every single day, Roger and I try, and sometimes fail, to be that example).

4. *It gives you a soft place to land at the end of the day.* Being married is tough, and dealing with kids and stepkids is even tougher. To survive, you need a rock-solid but cushy-soft place to land when things get unbearable. And a rock-solid but cushy place to flop when you have nowhere else to turn.

How do you know you're in a good "blended" marriage? When one of you says:

"Honey, I feel like running away."

And the other one replies, "That's fine. As long as you take me with you."

Your Marriage Is Different from a "Normal" Marriage

We've said before that it's important to accept your situation, to start where you are, and go from there. The reality is that your marriage is different from a "normal" marriage. Let me explain.

In a normal marriage, you had time together as a couple before you became a family.

In a normal marriage, you have only two adults weighing in on all kid issues.

In a normal marriage, when a child's textbook goes missing, it's probably buried in your child's room, not at Mom's house across town.

In a normal marriage, none of your children can say, "You're not my real mom."

In a normal marriage, none of your kids can ask to go live at Dad's house.

In a normal marriage, . . . Well, you get the picture.

Your marriage is not a normal marriage. You need to give yourself, and your spouse, extra grace in every situation.

But normal? It's overrated.

After being in a blended marriage, I feel like I can ride out anything. I'm smarter than I was ten years ago, I can get along with just about any personality type, and my stepkids call to come and hang out at our house.

I'd trade normal for that any day.

Remember, for Your Marriage, the Honeymoon Comes Later

Don't worry that you're being pathetic when you try not to get caught stealing a kiss from your spouse, or when you pray for a time when the kids are out of the house so you can make out on the couch, or when you consider a trip with your husband to the lawn-care section of Home Depot a hot date.

No. You're not pathetic. You're in a blended family. For us, it's three down, one to go. (Please don't ever tell my kids I wrote that.) That's the current count in our house. Three of our kids are out and living on their own. We have one to go, and then Roger and I will be in full-on honeymoon mode . . . for the rest of our lives.

Okay, so the honeymoon has already started in some small but significant ways. Since the last remaining child is an adult, Roger and I are free to go out when we want, travel when we want (with a built-in cat sitter), and not keep to a schedule. If we suddenly want to go out to dinner, this adult child can make his own mac 'n' cheese or reheat leftovers.

While "intact" families usually have a little time between the wedding night and the arrival of the first kiddo, blended families have a reverse timetable: We have all the kids with none of the alone time. Our "getting to know each other" happens in the midst of disciplining and organizing—and bathrooms that smell like cages at the local zoo.

But then we get to *really* look forward to the chance that we get to be alone for long stretches after the kids move out. While other moms are openly weeping as their babies drive off to college, I will kiss that last kid good-bye, dry the tear from my eye, and then promptly start making out with my husband on the living room couch!

COUPLE TIME IS NOT A LUXURY; IT'S NECESSARY FOR SURVIVAL

One of the huge (sometimes only) benefits to being in a blended family is that occasionally other people (the other parent, or possibly other relatives like your husband's ex in-laws) will take your child for a brief time. When Roger and I were first married, this didn't happen often, and I can't think of a time when both of the other parents had all our kids at the same time. But sometimes Roger and I were still able to get out of the house and leave the older kids in charge so that we could go have dinner, see a movie, or just run errands together.

Plus, my mom understood the need Roger and I had to be a couple.

So every few months, my mom and dad would land at our house and stay with the three younger kids, who were still living here. Mom couldn't just pop over for an evening (she lives almost three hours away), but she would come for a weekend so Roger could travel with me for work, or we could go out of town, just the two of us.

I know that not everyone has a sainted mother who will say, "Yes, let me take those puberty-laden children off your hands for two days while you run off to Tahoe," so we need to create the space if no one else will. There is always room for creativity.

My friend Tina and her husband set up their master bedroom like a bed-and-breakfast suite. They have a minifridge stocked with fancy water and sodas, chocolates, and cheese and crackers. They have Amazon Instant Video, and the best sheets they can afford. They call it their "retreat center," and the kids know that when the Do Not Disturb sign is up, they better not be knocking unless the house, or their sister, is on fire. About three times a week, Tina and her husband hang the sign on the bedroom door and just enjoy each other's company.

When Roger and I were first married, we found that the best time for us to connect was at lunchtime. We would each drive about halfway (around ten minutes) and have our alone dates at a dive Mexican restaurant or at a food truck at the park.

Another stepmom I know, Casey, makes sure that her travel for work never overlaps with the weekends her stepkids spend with their mom. If she has to travel, she does her best to make sure it's a time when her husband and the boys can be together. They go car camping or just go to their weekend games and then hang out afterward and watch boy movies. The boys appreciate having their dad to themselves, and Casey loves knowing that next weekend she gets her husband to herself.

How can you and your man get some alone time? Is there another blended family you can swap some babysitting with? Can you schedule a playdate or sleepover with all of your kids on the same night? Can you invite another couple over and put all the kids down so you can have some grown-up time? Can you plan babysitting into your weekly budget? After all the kids have gone to bed (or the older kids are settled for the night), can you set some time aside just for you and your husband?

Here are a few ideas:

- Curl up on the couch with your spouse and watch a favorite movie together (or just part of the movie each night over several nights).
- Have ice cream outside under the stars.
- Dance in your living room.
- Play a board game at the kitchen table.
- Go for a long walk (if you have older kids).

Here are some other marriage enhancing things you can do today to make life better for everyone in your home:

1. *Find some blended-family mentors.* I wish (oh, how I wish) Roger and I had found mentors in the stepparenting area sooner rather than later. Not just for the sake of our kids, but for the sake of our marriage.

If your church doesn't have a blended-family support group, then find another place that does. (In every group I've ever been to, they have been open to couples coming from other churches.) If you can't find a group, then start asking around at your own church. Find a family who has been doing this longer than you have, and ask them out to coffee or dinner. These people are your shortcut to a better marriage. When you confess that you've fought over the silliest things (carpool schedules, the kids' toothbrush habits, and so on), they will get it and possibly be able to top your silliest of arguments with some of their own.

There is real value in the blended-family world in being able to say, "Me, too!" or better yet, "Us, too!"

2. *Marital check-ins are critical.* Check in with each other. Do it causally and have a plan for it. Roger and I have our once-a-week

check-ins to go over schedules, talk about the kids, and more. But we also check in with each other to see how we're doing.

When Ben Affleck thanked his wife, Jennifer Garner, in his acceptance speech for winning Best Picture at the Oscars, he said, "I want to thank you for working on our marriage for ten Christmases." Affleck said to Garner from the stage, "It's good. It is work, but it's the best kind of work. And there's no one I'd rather work with."

And do you know what happened all over the Twitterverse? They blasted him.

"How can he say marriage is hard?"

"Boy, I bet he's in trouble tonight!"

"No one wants the world to know that their marriage is work!"

Really? Because who didn't get that memo? Marriage is hard. And the more we can admit it and be humble in our need for a loving God and a loving spouse, the better chance we have for this hard work to pay off.

3. *Honor your husband's kids.* You may think this is a piece of stepparenting advice, but really it's one of the most important pieces of marital advice I could give you. Treat his kids with kindness and respect at all costs.

This doesn't mean that you never set boundaries for your stepchildren or firmly remind them of the rules. What it does mean is that they are his kids, and you are in a role of supporting all of them in their relationships.

I know that I spent a lot of time trying to fit my stepkids into the mold I thought they should be in. I thought they needed to accept me, respect me, and love me. Then I realized that none of that was true. They did need to act accepting and respectful, but how they felt had to be developed over time. I couldn't force them, and I couldn't whine enough to Roger to make it happen. Stepfamilies meld at their own pace. We are the slow cookers of families. Trying to microwave the process only leaves everyone with a bad taste in their mouths.

When a man's kids are under attack, he can't help but want to come to their defense, even if the "attacker" is the woman he's promised to spend his whole life with. If your husband is constantly having to divide his loyalties, it's going to put a strain on your marriage, on him, and on you.

The last thing I want is for you and your husband to ever be on opposite sides of an argument when it comes to his kids. After several years, I finally learned how to approach Roger about these things. The best sample script I can share with you is this: "Roger, I want to have a great relationship with _____. Here is what I'm struggling with right now: _____. How do you think I should approach the situation?"

This statement accomplishes several things:

1. It immediately reminds my husband that I love his child.
2. It puts Roger and me on the same side of the situation.
3. It lets me share the issue with Roger without him feeling attacked.
4. It shows my husband I respect his opinion when it comes to his kids.

TALKING TO YOUR SPOUSE ABOUT HIS KIDS

Roger is my go-to guy . . . 98 percent of the time. But we stepmoms walk a fine line. If I'm having a frustrating time with one of my stepkids, Roger wants to hear about it and help, but I must remember one thing when I'm venting: These are his kids.

Think about this: If you are a mom, how do you feel when someone criticizes your kids? Even if it's someone who loves them dearly (your mom, your husband, a beloved teacher), it still hurts to hear someone talk about them in that way. It's the same for your husband.

I had dinner with a group of women the other night, and the conversation turned to stepparenting. One woman confided in me, "It's so weird. My husband has been in my son's life since he was five months old. He is the only father my son knows. But when my husband comes down on my son, it's different from when he is disciplining the other kids. I feel protective of my son."

From talking to other stepparents, this seems to be a common reaction. I know I feel it when Roger is frustrated with one of my kids. Plus, since Roger is such a peacekeeper at heart, he feels burdened with a sense that it's his responsibility to help everyone get along. So I've learned that with the big things, I always talk the issue over with Roger. The small stuff? That's where my friends come into the picture.

I have a few trusted friends—Erin, Michele, Susy, and Cheri—whom I share all my "mom stuff" with. We pray for each other's kids. We talk about parenting and, in Michele's case, stepparenting. It's not that I'm keeping anything from Roger. I'm just careful not to dump every little thought on him, every time I have one.

Not only does this make me a better mom; it makes me a better wife. Trying to get all my needs met by my husband is like trying to get all my shopping needs met by Target. Yep, Target can cover most areas (I mean who doesn't love a store where you can buy a bicycle chain and a silky teddy all on the same floor?), but no one place is designed to meet 100 percent of my needs. And my husband, while he may be great at listening when I feel like complaining about my work situation, may need a break from some of the kid drama.

So when I have hurt feelings, a small issue, or even—dare I say it—a gripe, I go to my girls and to God. My trusted girlfriends will hear me out, give me advice if I ask for it, and pray with me. Nine times out of ten, the issue is resolved without having to burden Roger with it.

Plus, so many men really do want to take care of their wives and kids by "fixing" the problem, while so many of us women just want someone to listen and understand. Go to whoever is going to give you what you need. Your girlfriends (the right ones) can give you the sympathy you want and the prayer you need without a list of to-dos attached.

I know you can do this. Yes, it's hard. But we want you to be married for a very long time to come, and part of that is getting super-creative about how, in the midst of some everyday struggles, you can have an extraordinary love affair with your husband.

TEN

Connected: Your Heart and God's

Let us then approach the throne of grace with

confidence, so that we may receive mercy and

find grace to help us in our time of need.

—HEBREWS 4:16

Is any one of you in trouble? He should pray.

—JAMES 5:13

Carol

I thought I was dying. So I prayed.

I know what you're thinking: You're about to read a story of miraculous healing. Well, yes and no. You decide.

The faces and reports of the doctors suggested that death was a real possibility, so I asked the Lord to save my life, but not because I was afraid to die. I trusted Jesus. I knew I'd be with Him. Nor was my greatest concern for my husband. He had already buried one wife, and while it would be sad for him to do it again, I knew he would be fine. The Lord had sustained him before, and He would do it again.

He had healed Jim's sorrow and even provided him with another wife. Plus, look at Ben Cartwright. We had grown up watching him on the TV show *Bonanza*. Ben had buried three wives and still managed to live a full, productive life on the Ponderosa with his three sons.

When I realized I might die, my greatest concern was for my girls. When we first got married, Jim and I decided it would be best for our family if I stayed home with Abby. It meant leaving a job I enjoyed and an income we appreciated, but I soon discovered my new "profession" of stay-at-home mom was my favorite. The extra time with Abby strengthened our bonding process, as Jim and I had prayed it would. I loved Abby. And when God blessed us with Allison and then Andrea, we were over the moon.

So when faced with the possibility of not being the one to teach them good manners, or how to treat people, or how to enjoy life, or—most important—about Jesus, it broke my heart. And I didn't want Abby crying over the grave of another mommy.

"Nobody else can love them like I do, Lord," I cried. While I usually possess a keen sense of the obvious, this time the irony that I was rearing someone else's child, and thus someone else could rear mine, escaped me. I continued, "Nobody else would rear them like I want to. Please save me, not only for my sake, but for theirs."

It didn't take but a minute to get a reply.

"So, Carol," God answered (not audibly but in my heart), "you trust that I have enough power to raise you from the dead when I return (John 6:40; 2 Corinthians 4:14), but you're not sure I can take care of the children I gave you? You know they really are *My* children, and I can rear them whether you are on the scene or not."

Well, when He put it like that . . .

I hadn't realized that all three of my children—no matter who gave birth to them—were someone else's. They were—and still are—*God's*.

WHOSE KIDS ARE THESE?

To borrow a line from *The Blues Brothers* movie, "We're on a mission from God,"[1] dear stepmom, to build good things into our stepchildren's lives. Thinking of stepchildren primarily as God's children makes all the difference. It affects how you think about them, how you speak to them, how you act toward them, and how you pray for them. It's the bottom line.

Note to reader: As it turns out, I didn't die. Apparently if you eat too many nuts and seeds while hiking the Grand Canyon, the consequent excruciating, two-week pain (and other symptoms too indelicate to mention here) can mimic more serious ailments. Also, doctors apparently run tests first sometimes and ask questions later. Questions like, "Have you eaten a lot of nuts and seeds lately?"

But God used those nuts and seeds to teach me an important lesson. My trust in Him grew as I yielded to Him yet again the lives and care of my children—um, *His* children—whom He had so graciously shared with me. And since they were His children, I learned not to pray that He would fill in the gaps of my parenting, but that He would rear my children through me. I'm just thankful He let me be a part of it.

A miraculous healing? Probably not the kind you (or I) expected, but a supernatural intervention nonetheless. God cured my thinking.

This is how Jesus wants us to view our stepchildren—as *His* children. This works well both for them and for us. It is so freeing!

I also learned that the best way to cooperate with my own prayer was by—wait for it—praying!

THIS IS FOR YOU

Prayer is so important for stepmoms. It's what will see us through. Perhaps you've been praying all your life. Or perhaps you have little or no experience with prayer. Perhaps you are like Sandra Bullock's character in the movie *Gravity*, where she says, "I've never prayed in my life. Nobody ever taught me how."[2] I don't want that to be you, dear stepmom. So no matter what your background or familiarity with prayer, this chapter is for you.

Stepmoms have plenty to discuss with God, but before we bare our hearts to someone, we want to know a little about whom we are talking to. Over the years, I've discovered I can be completely honest with God because He loves me and is trustworthy. I've come to realize that He neither judges me nor puts pressure on me to perform. I've learned I can pray a perfect prayer when I stop struggling with my prayer life and turning it into a "work." So can you. This is great news, because the last thing we need is more stress, more pressure, or one more thing to worry about. Prayer is part of our freedom.

We don't need perfect words or even a perfect motive to pray a perfect prayer. This is good news, because our motives are often selfish and self-centered. The prayer is perfect because of the One who hears it and in whose name it is prayed, not the one who prays it. It's more about His heart than our effort. Whew!

And if your motive isn't so perfect? He'll help you with that, too. Don't let it keep you from Him. And if you find yourself being tempted to or having an impulsive thought to harm your children, stepchildren, or yourself, tell God *and* a counselor right away. Both will help you. Remember, it is not a sin to experience temptation, only to act on it. Temptation is somewhat like physical pain: both are God's built-in warning mechanisms to alert us to the fact that something is wrong and we need to tend to the problem in order to prevent further hurt or injury. The support of a professional counselor is invaluable in this case. He or she can provide assistance and guidance from a neutral perspective.

Because God loves you, He will listen without condemning. He won't think less of you when you need to unload, even if it's a whine, and He won't put you on hold, either. You can relax in God's presence because He loves you. He delights in you. You are the apple of His eye. Just let that sink in for a moment and then keep reading. He is happy to hear from you. He is kind. He is wise. He understands you. He forgives you. He is trustworthy, and nothing can ever persuade Him to be otherwise. He will guide you in grace. He will remind you of truth. He will calm your fears. He will save you. He will sustain you. He will help you think straight. He will encourage you.

WOMAN AT THE WASHER

I distinctly remember the day I learned that lesson. One encounter with God at the washing machine changed my whole perception of His response to me. I felt like a modern-day "woman at the well" because there I was, going about my daily mundane chores, and the next thing I knew, BAM! I was face-to-face with the compassion, grace, and encouragement of Jesus.

I was bubbling with irritation at someone, a condition common to many stepmothers. As I loaded the washer, I ranted to the Lord, "I can't stand what she's doing!" I expected God to reprimand me ("You shouldn't feel that way") or patronize me with a "There, there," or at least be disappointed in me for feeling that way. Instead, He condemned neither me nor my irritation but reminded me, from the verse that had been rolling around in my mind all morning, that He didn't like this person's behavior either, and He was on the job. He also reminded me to keep on doing what I knew to do, and to remember that He was telling me to do it. That's a lot of reminding from one verse—"Overcome evil with good" (Romans 12:21).

I love that God will do that for us as we meditate on His Word. I love that nothing is too small to bring to Him, that He wants to be involved in everything that concerns me because He loves me. Honestly, prayer is the only way I have been able to lose sixty pounds and keep them off for more than thirty years. I have prayed over every morsel that has crossed my lips before ever getting out of bed. One of my stepmom friends didn't think her weight was worthy of bringing before the Lord. It is. She thought God had bigger and more important things to tend to, and she didn't want to bother Him. But she was no bother to God—and neither are you!

The stresses and pressures of stepfamily life can tempt us to cope in unhealthy ways. God certainly does care, and He welcomes our prayers. Remember, He even knows the number of hairs on your head (Matthew 10:30), a number that changes daily from what scientists (and our hairbrushes) tell us. But really, who knows the *exact* number? Only God. What do *we* know? That He wants to be involved in every aspect of our lives—and our stepfamilies' lives.

When I say that God spoke to me—in this story and others—I am not saying I heard an actual voice. I experienced an inner leading of His Spirit. When you pray and sense a similar response, be sure the answer you sense is in agreement with Scripture. That way you know it's legitimate. God will never contradict Himself by telling you something different from what He has already said in His Word. Scripture is God speaking to us, where He begins the conversation. It's where we get to know Him. It's where He reveals His thoughts, His heart, His desires, His dreams, His plans, and His love for us. God is a good conversationalist. We respond in prayer and keep the conversation going.

We Speak, We Listen

"Prayer is listening to the heartbeat of God," says pastor and Fuller Theological Seminary professor Dr. James A. Graham. "It is me calming down so His understanding becomes mine. We pray because we can. It is both a privilege and a commandment."

Prayer is our lifeline. It is our oxygen. It connects us to the wisest, most loving, and powerful Person in the universe. I can speak only for myself, but I need this. I suspect that you do too. And sometimes we need help getting there.

One blended family I know discovered prayer as their great unifier. Mike and Sara knew prayer was important to them individually and as a couple, and they wanted it to be important to their children and stepchildren as well. Mike and Sara already prayed together for each member of their family in the mornings before they both left for work, and they ended their days together the same way. Now they wanted to pray together as a family. They tried prayer at the dinner table, but the nights when they all ate together were rare, since their teenagers had football practice and part-time jobs.

They tried bedtime prayers but found only their younger children were open to that. But they stuck with it, asking God to show them a way to connect with Him and each other in prayer. Through trial and error, they developed a system that worked. Sara posted a prayer-request sheet on the refrigerator, where everyone could write down his or her need or praise. Each person would date and sign the prayer request, and as other family members read it, they would initial it, showing they were aware and praying. When an answer came, the person who originally posted the request would add it to the paper. Other family members could then draw a happy face by it or write a comment in response.

This process built relationships within the family and gave them extra reasons to celebrate. It proved easier (and seemed less threatening and less vulnerable to the kids) to write down their prayer requests rather than say them aloud and have to look at each other's faces, especially in the beginning. Like most aspects of blended-family life, it took awhile for everyone to become comfortable with this approach, but Mike and Sara's Prayer Poster strengthened their family's bond with God and with each other. They loved it and now recommend it to other blended families.

Refreshing Prayer

"Often when I am under stress and pressure, I feel one of my greatest needs is to get a good night's sleep. But I've found that physical rest alone is not enough to revive my flagging spirit. I need the spiritual revival that comes from spending quiet time alone with Jesus in prayer and in thoughtful meditation on His Word. . . . Could some of the exhaustion you are feeling be the result of simple prayerlessness?"[3] writes Anne Graham Lotz.

My response? "Yes, Anne, it certainly could be. It's definitely one option. Because, sometimes, I confess, I don't feel like praying." Do you ever feel that way?

It's normal—and okay—not to feel like praying. Sometimes you might not feel like praying for a particular person. It's normal to think, *I don't even like so-and-so (insert the person's name here), and I don't feel like praying for her (or him).* So you don't. Understandable and normal, but not helpful, either to so-and-so or you. Here's why: When Jesus tells us to pray, it's because He loves us, and it benefits us to pray. When we do, we are blessed beyond what we can imagine. And often as we pray, our feelings change. But even if they don't, we will still be blessed. We don't have to like the people we pray for.

"I've found that the best way to turn anger, bitterness, hatred, and resentment for someone into love is to pray for that person. God softens your heart when you do,"[4] writes Stormie Omartian in *Lord, I Want to Be Whole.*

I have good news for you: When you pray for someone, you are giving love to that person. No *feelings* of love required. Jesus said, "Pray for those who mistreat you. . . . Love your enemies, do good to them. . . . Then your reward will be great, and you will be sons of the Most High, because he is kind to the ungrateful" (Luke 6:28, 35). Even if people in your stepfamily aren't your enemies, sometimes they may seem like it because of their actions. But Jesus says to pray for them, not because they're so great, but in response to His great love . . . for you. He says it's while you're praying for and showing kindness to those who are ungrateful that you are most like your heavenly Father. And He is the One who rewards you.

So we pray for others because Jesus loves us. And prayer works when we know we're loved. Every day He makes our character more like His. You may not feel like it, but you are a great lover in this world, dear stepmom. You got into this whole situation because of love. And you are one person through whom Jesus wants to show His love to your stepchildren. One way is through prayer. The other is praise.

GET YOUR PRAISE ON

Praise is always appropriate, no matter what your current circumstances. "Let everything that has breath praise the LORD. [That's us!] Praise the LORD," writes the psalmist in Psalm 150:6. And Scripture is full of reasons why.

But how do you start, and what if you get stuck?

A great place to start is by praying God's words back to Him. When you have no words of your own, pray God's words back to Him. When His words express your heart, pray God's words back to Him. When you need the power and wisdom of His words, pray God's words back to Him. Here are a few suggestions of what to pray for:

- *Pray for wisdom.* James 1:5 says, "If any of you lacks wisdom . . ." Could this be you? Good. It certainly describes me. Because the verse goes on to say, ". . . he should ask God, who gives generously to all without finding fault, and it will be given to him." Great news! God will always give you wisdom when you ask.

- *Pray for the ability to "consider it pure joy . . . whenever you face trials of many kinds"* (James 1:2). Uh-huh. But don't worry about this. Since God tells you to do it, His love will empower you to do it. And watch what it does for your attitude!

- *Pray for patience.* It's *good* to pray for patience. You read that right. Some say never pray for patience because God will put you in situations where you need it. You, darling stepmom, are *already* in those kinds of situations. *Of course* pray for patience. It's a fruit of God's Spirit within you, along with love, joy, peace, kindness, goodness, faith, gentleness, and self-control (Galatians 5:22–23). Those are all good things.

  I've learned that patience actually means what you do while you're waiting—remaining consistently the same whether you're in a particularly stressful situation or not. Everyone waits. Patience comforts you while you wait. God wants you to be hope-filled and gracious while you wait, and He will enable you to do it.

In addition to these suggestions, I'm sure you'll think of other needs as you pray for yourself specifically. And let's pray for each other as stepmothers. I'm already praying for you.

BUSY STEPMOMS PRAY

Stepmoms are busy. Do you feel too busy to pray? When you're pressed for time, anything is better than nothing. Got five minutes? Pray. One minute? Go for it. Time for one word only? Breathe out "Father" and watch God run to you in response. He doesn't despise your day of "small things" (Zechariah 4:10). Often, the more you pray, the more you'll want to pray. If finding time is an issue, ask God for help.

Author and speaker Anne Ortlund writes that when she had three children under the age of three, the only time she had to herself was in the middle of the night. She told God that if He would restore the energy she lost by getting up in the wee hours to spend time with Him, she would meet with Him between two and three every morning. He did, and she did. "I'm not sorry I did it,"[5] she writes in *Disciplines of the Beautiful Woman*.

Find whatever works for you. Like Anne, you won't be sorry.

STEPFAMILY PRAYERS

While you're at it, pray for your stepfamily's specific needs. We need to be strong and courageous on our stepmother journey. Prayer is one way to get there.

Our husbands need prayer not only for their physical, mental, spiritual, and emotional needs but also for their roles—husband, father, possibly stepfather. Following are some suggestions:

- Pray that your husband will adjust to his roles in your step-family, feel confidence in his ability to succeed in them, and understand the adjustments everyone else is making as well.
- Pray that he will relate with wisdom and kindness to each of his children (and yours, if you bring them into the marriage).
- Pray that he will be sensitive to your needs as a stepmother, and that God will give him wisdom to help meet those needs. (Note: You can make it easier for your husband by clueing him in on what your needs are and even offering tips for ways he can help meet them. Do you need some alone time, for example? Let him know. Just don't act moody, withdraw, or snip at him. Let him know.)

- Pray that he will be sensitive to the leading of the Holy Spirit. (And remember, that's not you.)

Our children and stepchildren need our prayers as well. In addition to all the usual issues children face, children in stepfamilies have unique needs. Consider the following suggestions:

- Pray that they will feel loved and accepted by God and their stepfamily, especially you.
- Pray that they will adjust to being in a stepfamily and accept each member of it, especially you.
- Pray that they will learn to get along with each member of their stepfamily. Reassure stepsiblings they don't have to love each other, but you do expect them to treat each other with respect, at least as well as they would treat the neighbors.[6]
- Pray that you will use wisdom in dealing with their personal issues. Ask your husband to tell you about his children individually and share with him your observations. (Be careful not to criticize them or how they've been parented.) If they don't know Jesus personally, that is their greatest need.

Let Your Family Know You Pray for Them

I wanted every member of my family to know I prayed specifically for them and kept a prayer journal to jot down their requests, as well as my own petitions for them. Of course, physical safety always made the list.

While attending college and living at home, Abby worked full-time at an outlet mall twenty miles away. I let her know I prayed daily for her safety on the highway, along with other concerns. (Of course, one of those concerns was for Jim and me not to worry about her spending so much time on the road.)

One evening she came home aflutter, her wide eyes and rapid speech saying it all even before she had a chance to tell us how she had barely avoided being involved in a six-car pileup on the freeway. Her heart was still pounding. We all thanked God that night with extra fervor for Abby's safety. And as a bonus, when Abby knew she was covered in prayer, it helped her see both my love and concern for her and that of her heavenly Father's.

If your stepkids are open to the idea, let them know you pray for them regularly. Ask them for specific requests and let them know when you see God's answers. If it's a sore point with them now, keep it to yourself and save it for later, when they may be more receptive. Either way, *you* will enjoy it.

Any exes, in-laws, and extended-family members need a spot on your prayer list too, especially if (when) they have offended you. Of course, you also want to pray for yourself. This is good, because no detail of your life is too insignificant. As a stepmom, you have individual needs as well as specific prayer requests for your marriage:

- For trust and unity, and that God will knit your hearts together.
- For healing of memories.
- For insight into your mate and children/stepchildren.
- For strength, courage, endurance, and renewed commitment for those days you think, *I don't want to do this anymore.*

Not sure what you need? Ask God to show you; then ask Him for whatever it is you need. And remember to thank Him. If something is lacking in your relationship, remember that Jesus can give you and your husband whatever you need.

PRAYING FOR YOURSELF AS A STEPMOM

The happiest stepmoms ask God . . .

- to help us not be easily offended, and to be quick to forgive when we are. As well as quick to seek forgiveness when we are the offenders.

- to give us the ability to set and respect healthy boundaries.
- to enable us to believe we have what God says we have: His leading as our good Shepherd, the mind of Christ, self-control, and peace, as well as the ability to experience it.

Short words and short prayers work fine. Jesus never condemned short prayers, but He did warn against using many words. Even when Jesus performed one of His most magnificent miracles by raising Lazarus from the dead, notice how short and to the point His prayer was (see John 11:41–42). In it, He gave us two keys to effective prayer: (1) He acknowledged God as His Father, and (2) He thanked God for hearing Him. Then after praying, He acted.

"Jesus taught a model prayer, the Lord's Prayer, but otherwise gave few rules. His teaching reduces down to three general principles: *Keep it honest, keep it simple, and keep it up.* Mainly, Jesus pressed home that we come as beloved children to a Father who loves us in advance and cares deeply about our lives,"[7] author Philip Yancey writes.

ONCE IS ENOUGH

You don't need to keep repeating the same thing over and over or come at it from every possible angle. I have a tendency to do this in human conversation, to make sure everybody understands what I'm trying to say. It drives my daughters crazy. They've borrowed a system a friend developed of raising one finger (not the middle one!) when I'm saying something they've heard before. When they flex all fingers at the same time, it reminds me they've heard this a thousand times, and they "get it." God hears you the first time, and though it never drives Him crazy to hear it again, He gets it. Rest assured He is already at work on your behalf. And remember to thank Him.

Here are some helpful guidelines to keep in mind when you pray:

- *Pray continually.* I'm not making this up (see 1 Thessalonians 5:17). How do we do that? It doesn't even sound realistic, so sometimes we brush aside the idea. I know I have. Yet really, in simple terms, it means living a lifestyle of continual awareness of God and His goodness, acknowledging that our Father loves us, hears us, and blesses us through the finished work of Jesus. We remember and remind ourselves that we can trust His heart.
- *Express thanks to God.* First Thessalonians 5:18 tells us to "give thanks in all circumstances, for this is God's will for you in Christ Jesus." We thank God, knowing that "in all things God works for the good of those who love him" (Romans 8:28). We thank God even in the midst of terrifying, frustrating circumstances, knowing He will ultimately bring good out of them for us.
- *Pray with your church family during worship.*
- *Pick a verse to think about all day.* Turn it around and around in your mind. Pray about it, asking God to reveal what it means and to fill you with understanding and wisdom through it.

KEEP FIRST THINGS FIRST

I learned this lesson in a dramatic way. I had established a daily schedule that matched my priorities of first honoring God and centering my heart in Him and then exercising for my health before launching into the day's activities. I did pretty well for a while. Like the Israelites of old, I "gathered my manna" in the morning through prayer and Bible study and then slid into my sneakers to hit the treadmill.

One day, for no good reason (except that I have sheep-like tendencies to wander off on my own ill-chosen path), I started to reverse the order. As I laced up my jogging shoes—not that I actually jogged, but that's what the box said—I sensed God asking in a kind, not condemning, tone, "Where do you think you're going?"

"Um . . . nowhere!" I answered as I kicked off my shoes and opened my Bible.

First things first.

Even if you're not a morning person, even if you're rushed for time, take a few minutes before you get out of bed to renew your mind by handing over to God any critical, angry, fearful, or anxious thoughts. Then picture yourself receiving from Him love, grace, peace, joy, and wisdom in exchange. Let them soak in. Set your mind to receive those good things from Him all day. Thank Him. Praise Him for who He is and then enjoy a moment of worship, letting His love fill you. Now your feet are ready to hit the floor.

(As unique as we all are, you may find it more convenient or productive to pray and study at a different time of day or night. You have the freedom to do that! Whatever works best for you, and it might even change with the different seasons of your life.)

Prayer is a valuable use of your time. It will change your heart. It will change your life.

One night after I had tucked in six-year-old Andrea with a Bible story, a song, and a prayer, I walked past her bedroom and heard her laughing. I couldn't resist poking my head in through the doorway and asking her what was going on.

"I'm just telling God some jokes," she said.

She gets it.

ELEVEN

Building Trust

Trust in the LORD with all your heart

and lean not on your own understanding;

in all your ways acknowledge him, and

he will make your paths straight.

—PROVERBS 3:5–6

Kathi and Carol

Jeremy spent a lot of time not speaking to me (Kathi).

I remember one day when Roger called me from work and asked if I could take Jeremy to hockey practice. The funny thing was, Jeremy was in the very next room and had just called his dad at work. Roger then called me at home to ask if I could take *the kid in the next room* to practice.

There was, however, one conversation Jeremy and I had every single day. It was the "What's for dinner?" conversation. Jeremy would arrive home from school, and the only question he would ask was, "What's for dinner?" I have to tell you, I was so resentful every single time he asked. *How dare you ask about dinner when you can't even be nice to me?* That was the feeling in my tiny, shriveled-up, apple-left-in-the-sun heart.

After several months of this, I started to notice a different reaction from Jeremy. When I told him, "We're having pork chops and kale for dinner," he would respond with one word: "Cool."

But if I said, "Oh, it's been a busy day. I think we're going to order pizza tonight," or "Your dad said he was going to pick up something from the store," Jeremy would just grunt in that teenage-boy way of his.

I was flummoxed. Jeremy never said he liked my cooking, but he always seemed disappointed when I wasn't making dinner. What I came to discover was that it wasn't that Jeremy necessarily wanted my cooking; he just wanted *someone* cooking for him.

Roger had been an amazing single dad. Getting two kids to two different schools and activities, volunteering at church, and keeping the whole brood fed and clothed is a pretty amazing feat for a couple, but for a single dad? That's superhero status right there. Yet while Roger was (and is) a great cook, there just wasn't time to get meals on the table and do everything else he needed to do. So his meal plan usually consisted of a debit card and yelling into a drive-thru speaker.

But there was something inside Jeremy that longed to have a dinner made for him every night. There was something about routine and consistency that Jeremy needed in his life, which I was offering.

When Roger and I came to this conclusion, we both worked harder to get dinner on the table. Kudos to Roger for stepping up after a long day of work and barbecuing about twice a week while I tried to take the rest of the days. Oh, sure, we still had pizza from the little shop around the corner (Mom and Dad needed a break every once in a while!), but for the most part, we realized that Jeremy needed the consistency, and we did too.

Dinner may seem like a small thing, but in our house, it was a big step to building trust in our stepfamily. Building trust in our stepfamilies—between us and our stepkids, between us and our partners—is a huge factor in gaining the kind of family we are hoping for. I look at it this way: Trust has already been broken in your stepchild's life.

Whether your husband and his former wife parted ways through divorce or death, your stepchild has experienced pain and brokeness. I'm not blaming anyone, but it's the truth. And part of my job as a loving stepmom is giving my stepkids a trustworthy relationship with me.

For years I thought the main goal of being a stepmom—the thing that would make all of our lives so much easier—was getting my stepkids to like me and know how much I liked them. But now I've come to understand that what they needed most from me were two things: someone to respect and someone to trust. They needed to know these things as well:

- That when I said I was going to do something (pick them up from an event, cook a special dinner, pick something up from the store), I would do it.
- That when I asked them to do a chore, I would follow through and not let it go because I wanted to keep the peace.
- That when Roger and I made a promise to them about a trip or an event, we would follow through.

Consistency. That's what my stepkids needed from me. And that terrified me, since consistency isn't my strong suit. I'm a "fun mom." I love to play games and be silly with my kids. We love to hang out together. But consistency? I bristle at the very word.

But before my stepkids could really have fun with me, they needed to be able to trust me. So we had chore charts and schedules, menus and shopping lists. Yep, I could fake consistency.

And eventually it did work. We even started to have regular dinner-and-game nights that all the kids participated in, even the ones who'd moved out of the house. And we've kept that up ever since.

I really believe that as with any relationship, trust is built up over time with hundreds, if not thousands, of tiny, faithful acts. So where there is a bump in the road (such as being late for a pickup or not being able to help with homework like you promised because of an emergency), there's a better chance of grace. I also think that our ability to show trustworthiness springs from an ability to increase our trust in God during the harder times of stepparenting.

Being a stepmom means developing a new set of skills. Like learning any new skill, it's going to look messy as we're learning and growing. And like a little girl who is learning to ride a bike and leans on her daddy to make sure she doesn't fall, we, too, have to lean on our heavenly Father to make sure we don't metaphorically face-plant in the neighbor's bushes.

Being a stepmom requires asking for grace over and over again. I stand up, I fall down, I try again. I've often had to ask for grace from my husband, my kids, and my stepkids. I've had to ask for help from all of them as well. And I know that in my own journey, the more I can trust God with my failings, the more hope I have for a better future as a stepmom.

I (Carol) often prayed for love and trust to grow between Abby and me at each stage of her life, and I sought ways to encourage both to happen. I knew one way was treating all of my children with the same love and care. I constantly tried to be "fair," particularly in the amount of time and attention I gave to each child, but it was difficult due to the big gap in their ages.

A baby and a preschooler obviously require (and usually want) more time and attention from a parent than does a teenager. Since Abby was at school about eight hours a day, I worked hard to find ways to include her in activities with the younger two girls. Sometimes it worked, but sometimes it backfired, like when she understandably didn't want to do the same things the "littles" needed to do, or they were too young to participate in her activities.

Sometimes it seemed like a losing battle, but I learned that "fair" doesn't mean "exactly the same." While it does mean each child gets approximately the same number and dollar amount of gifts at Christmas, it doesn't necessarily mean that when one child needs a new pair of shoes, everybody gets a new pair of shoes.

Turning to God in prayer gave Jim and me some great ideas for growing both love and trust in our blended family. By taking turns staying with the younger ones (and enjoying grandparents' offers to babysit), Jim and I each dedicated one-on-one time to spend with Abby in her choice of activities. Jim served as the sole male on Abby's Girl Scout troop's whale-watching expedition to San Diego. (He provided protection and an impromptu mini-education on more than sea life when their hotel surprisingly wound up across the street from a motel that charged by the hour.)

Abby and I roughed it together, sleeping in tents on a "mom and me" Girl Scout weekend. (If that doesn't say love, I don't know what does!) I also served as homeroom mother during her grade-school years, and Jim volunteered as church camp counselor. Eventually we started letting Abby invite a friend to join us on vacation, so she and her friend could have fun together while Jim and I were occupied with the demands of the younger set. It also allowed Jim and me to spend some focused time with Abby and her friend after the little ones went to bed. We became quite adept at playing Clue and Taboo and could qualify as card sharks.

Many of those ideas worked great, but certainly not all of them. When the girls were young and I still had full control over what they wore, on special occasions like Easter, I enjoyed dressing Allison and Andrea alike (including ruffled socks and massive hair bows), a look I thought was adorable but have come to find out not everyone else does. (By "everyone else," I mean the now grown-up Allison and Andrea.) I wanted Abby to feel included, but she didn't want to wear those outfits, and who could blame her? But I didn't give up. I soon got an idea of something we could all enjoy doing together—and look good while we were doing it. I searched stores and catalogs for matching outfits that looked appropriate for all ages so we Boley girls could have our picture taken as a surprise for Jim.

Now *that* sounded fun to everyone. But do you know how hard it is to find something an eighteen-month-old, a five-year-old, a teenager, and an almost-forty-year-old mom look good in? (Except for University of Arizona T-shirts, of course—"Bear Down, Wildcats!"—but Jim's an Arizona State fan, so that was a no-go.) I finally stumbled across some matching sweaters that looked decent, and off we drove to the photographer's.

There I was with my big eighties hair, corralling toddler Andrea. There was Abby sporting her enormous eighties eyeglasses, and there was Allison in her sweater and huge, matching hair ribbon. Jim was surprised, all right. We could have passed for one of those family-portraits-from-the-big-box-chain-store photos circulating on the Internet. I wanted to show family unity, solidarity. Perhaps an epic fail at the time, but a big laugh now every time we look at it. Every. Time. I'm giggling even now! Maybe it worked after all.

And I do know this—just the fact that I made the effort to do things together showed Abby my intentions and my heart and helped build trust between us, as I had prayed it would. God answered that prayer with a lovely "Yes," as He continued to build my trust in Him. I thanked Him then, and I still thank Him. He's a great God.

Trusting God in the Hard Times

Because we are "steps," it means that there has been a big break in our lives. Breaks in marriages, breaks in relationships, breaks in trust—not just with our families, but with God. Even though I (Kathi) made mistakes in my first marriage, I got the basics right, and I thought as long as I was doing everything I was supposed to do, God would honor that. So when it came time for my marriage to end, I wasn't just upset with my husband; I was mad at God. I felt as if I had been gypped out of the family I'd worked for. I felt that I was cheated out of the family I deserved.

Trusting God wasn't something I'd had a lot of practice with. In my mind, I figured that if I worked hard, good things should happen. That's the opposite of trusting God. So when I became a single mom, I broke up with God for a while. Okay, maybe we didn't break up, but we were "taking a break." (Yes, you would be correct in guessing that I was the only one taking a break.) I thought that if God really cared for me, He wouldn't let me go through the pain I was experiencing.

Yet it was during those times as a single mom that God met me in my pain. He sent people to encourage me, words to embolden me, and money to keep us going. Even when I didn't feel like my needs (or wants) were being met, I was starting to develop a deep trust in God and His provision. Because I'd seen Him come through so many times before, I was starting to see that I could trust Him with my future, even when I didn't understand it.

As stepmoms, we have a unique role that enables us to experience God's love and care and trust Him in a way many others don't get to. As a mom, I had some control over my kids when they were younger. My control as a stepmom was very limited, but my influence through prayer, my behavior, and my attitude was almost limitless.

And that caused me to trust God in bigger and better ways.

Let's be honest, control is an illusion most of the time, even with our own kids. But with my stepkids, any illusions of control evaporated very quickly, and I knew that my biggest influence in many ways was to not only trust God with my stepkids but to demonstrate trusting God.

Here are some of the concrete ways I was able to demonstrate trusting God with my stepkids:

- *I reminded my husband of God's care for his children.* Of course, my husband would get down about his kids. Every parent does. But as something of an outsider (in a good way), I could be more objective about Roger's kids and their talents. When you're a parent, every disappointment feels like the end of the world. But as a stepmom, I was more easily able to take the long view of Jeremy's and Amanda's bumps along the road to growing up. (And Roger is a master of this with my kids.)

  When Jeremy came home with a failing grade in his college math class, Roger was understandably upset. But I know Jeremy, and I could separate myself from the disappointment. I reminded Roger what a hard worker Jeremy is, and how if he really wanted to pass that class, he would. That class turned out to be the biggest obstacle Jeremy has ever faced academically. He took that class five times at three different schools, but finally he passed with a B-plus!

- *I was the family scribe.* We have a bunch of rocks in our backyard that we wrote on with Sharpie markers. We would write things on the rocks like "Amanda's Promotion. God's Faithfulness! August 2014." As a family, we wanted to remember all the things God had done for us, so like the Ebenezer stones in the Old Testament, we remembered God's faithfulness with stones of remembrance in our backyard. Not only was it a great reminder for our kids, but it also reminded me of all the ways God cared for our kids.

- *I reminded my stepkids that I pray for them all the time.* Not only did this practice up my trust in God; it upped my relationship with my kids. It's hard to stay frustrated or annoyed with someone you're praying for. (And I know that this helped me be less frustrating and annoying as well.)

- *I came to terms with my lack of control.* Once I truly got to the place where I realized that my stepkids were going to do less listening to what I said and pay more attention to what I *did*, it was a game changer. I had no control over my stepkids, only influence.

Here are two more ways I was able to demonstrate trusting God to my stepkids.

- *I stopped trying to be in control all the time.* As my kids and stepkids were growing up, I tried to micromanage the details of their lives so they would never make any mistakes. But as my friend Cheri, one of the most thorough and intentional people I know, put it so well, "How did I learn to plan ahead? From my mother's reminders, or from experiencing the consequences of failing to plan ahead?" I had to trust God to let the members of my family fail. How would they learn to take care of themselves if I was constantly running in front of them clearing a path and laying pillows down, refusing to ever let them fall?

  Doesn't God care for my kids more than I do? I need to trust Him with them every day—not just with my words, but with my actions as well. More important, this shows my whole family that I trust God with the big things: them.

- *Roger and I shared our struggles with our kids.* No, our kids were not privy to every fight, argument, and disagreement Roger and I had. But when there was (or is) a big issue in our lives (financial, health, relational), we let our kids know, and we let them know we were praying about it. I love nothing more than getting to brag on God to our kids. I want Him to be real in their lives as well as ours.

  About four years into our marriage, Roger and I hit a big financial snag. Okay, more than a snag. There was a huge tear in our finances. And we were desperate. We didn't know how we were going to make our next house payment, pay our employees, or even get groceries. It was a pretty desperate time. Our kids knew that things were bad. We'd had a family discussion about our need to tighten our belts, but now we had a flat-out stoppage of outgoing money. No sports, no clothes, nothing. So we asked our kids to pray.

One evening Roger and I were out taking one of our habitual walks, and we were praying. (To be honest, Roger was the one praying. I was crying.) That's when Roger had a thought. There was an account he'd started paying into about nine years earlier through his work. He'd decided to take it off his financial radar so he wouldn't be tempted to spend it. In fact, it was so far off his radar, he'd completely forgotten about it.

At exactly the right time, God brought to Roger's mind exactly the solution we needed. Our kids knew how worried we were, but they also knew how committed we were to trusting God in the situation. So we told them about God's answer to our prayers. And they got an up-close-and-personal view of God providing for our family in powerful ways.

Building trust with our stepkids, it seems to me, means showing them whom we trust. When it's obvious we're learning trust from the One who is most trustworthy, our faith and commitment show our stepchildren (and the rest of our family) that we are growing in ways that will benefit the entire family.

TWELVE

Forgiveness: The Cure for Your Hurting Heart

Be kind and compassionate to one another, forgiving

each other, just as in Christ God forgave you.

—EPHESIANS 4:32

Carol

One scene still haunts me. I remember it in excruciating detail, and although it occurred a month before I officially became a stepmom, I consider it one of my biggest stepmom fails. Jim, Abby, and I were riding in his orange Ford Fiesta, affectionately called Fester, on our way to the mall so I could buy Abby a new Easter outfit. It would be a special gift from me to her. Bonding, you know.

Plans included a visit to the Easter Bunny for five-year-old Abby. I hadn't had children yet, and I wasn't "up" on these things. I assumed that by nearly six, she knew the scoop on the Easter Bunny, but listening to her talk from the backseat, I wasn't sure. Was she kidding, going along with the charade just for fun? I didn't understand. I was definitely at a disadvantage here. It was one thing Jim and I had failed to discuss about her upbringing. I didn't think the Easter Bunny was that big of a deal—certainly not in the same league as Santa—and I wanted her to know the truth. But instead of waiting to ask Jim in private, I blurted out, "Well, you know the Easter Bunny isn't real, right?"

No, she didn't. I could have torn my tongue out as she started to cry. It certainly wasn't my intention to be hurtful. Yet that's exactly what I had done. Jim shot me a look of disbelief and irritation. I usually was more thoughtful than this. What was I thinking? Obviously not much. I can't even tell you what an uncomfortable scene unfolded inside that car.

I felt like a *wicked almost-stepmother*. If only I could have taken back my words. Since we were buckled in, I couldn't put Abby on my lap to comfort her. I couldn't turn around in my seat far enough to even touch her. Jim could see how upset I was, and so in addition to disbelief and irritation, he also felt sorry for me. There was only one thing to do. I asked forgiveness of them both and begged for mercy.

It took awhile for everyone to regain control of themselves, but after some ice cream at the mall, a visit with the Easter Bunny (who we now knew was no bunny at all), and the joy of finding just the right Easter outfit for Abby, all was well in our world again.

To this day, I am still appalled at my lack of sensitivity every time I remember that story; however, I also rejoice in the fact that I am forgiven.

That incident taught me to be much more careful in my choice of words so, hopefully, I wouldn't go around offending small children (or adults) and wouldn't need forgiveness as often in that area. I've learned that whether you are the one needing it or the one granting it, forgiveness has the power to set you free. It's a beautiful thing.

It makes no difference where your sin or someone else's sin against you ranks on the Richter scale of offenses, forgiveness is the cure.

LOTS OF "SMALL" ISSUES

Not only are there times when we need forgiveness, but there are times when we have to offer forgiveness. Most stepmothers face smallish issues to forgive, but we face *lots* of them. Every day we're presented with at least fifty things that could offend us. But little things as well as "the biggies" can trip us up if not forgiven right away. Even when no intention to hurt exists, feelings get hurt. Talking through issues as they arise helps keep our slates—and our hearts—clean. It can be tempting to ignore those smaller issues, thinking they're no big deal or that we should be able to "just get over them," but small issues can build up and make us crazy while nobody else even realizes anything is wrong.

As Suzanne Eller writes in *The Unburdened Heart*, "Forgiving the small stuff is important because it is your day-to-day experiences that propel you forward or keep you stuck. They affect your heart, which affects your attitude, which affects your relationships, even your relationship with God."[1]

Be quick to forgive. Don't let the poison of unforgiveness stick around, strangling the life out of you. And when you forgive, don't magnify the offender's sin and throw it back in his or her face. Here's one of the most helpful tips on forgiveness: Decide before someone offends you that you will forgive. Identify yourself as a forgiver. You'll save yourself a lot of heartache that way.

AND SOME HUGE ISSUES

Remember Stacey's story in chapter 6? The one where her stepson, Daniel, never responded even once in more than twenty-five years to her consistent actions and overtures of love but then took her hand and skated wordlessly with her around the ice rink? She called it "a kiss from God." There's more to the story.

In spite of Daniel's actions, Stacey stayed diligent in being the kind of stepmother she wanted to be. She knew she didn't want to hold on to anger and bitterness, nor did she want to heap condemnation on Daniel. She understood Daniel's anger was that of a child disappointed about not being able to live with his father full-time, and she recognized Daniel's jealousy over a new half sibling. Stacey wanted to encourage Daniel to find positive ways to express his feelings, so she helped get him into counseling and learn constructive coping skills. She realized it would take time to see positive change—and it did take time, along with prayer, trusting God, and continuing to build trust with her stepson. But she eventually received her "kiss from God."

How was Stacey able to respond to Daniel with love and kindness? It started with her decision to forgive.

WHY IS FORGIVENESS SO IMPORTANT?

In the course of stepfamily life, we experience hurts that can cause us to become and stay bitter, angry, resentful, and sorry for ourselves. Here's the thing to remember: It will kill us if we do. And it will be death by suicide. Bitterness, anger, resentment, and self-pity are real. Each is a natural response to the way others mistreat us. And if we stay stuck in them, each is a choice we make. But what other choice do we have? Only one.

"Revenge?" you may ask. While revenge is tempting, it always falls short of what we want to accomplish. When we've been hurt, it's natural to want to hurt back, but when we take revenge, we hurt ourselves even more. Revenge backfires.

What other options do we have when our hearts hurt so badly and long for relief? Forgiveness. That's what the following stepmoms decided to do.

The biological mother of Patty's stepchildren lied about her to the children and then dumped them on her doorstep . . . permanently, leaving Patty to deal not only with their full-time care but also with their rejection. In spite of this, the children defended their mother and resented Patty for years. And yet after Patty decided to forgive her stepchildren's biological mother and the children themselves, she was able to treat them all with grace and respect. Patty went about fulfilling her daily responsibilities to the children—chauffeuring them to music lessons, sporting events, doctor's appointments, and dental checkups; preparing meals; making sure they were ready for school; and teaching them personal hygiene. Over time the children grew to respect her, and she even had the privilege of leading them to Jesus. It started with her decision to forgive.

When Sandy's stepchildren spoke and acted disrespectfully toward her, her husband never defended her because he was afraid to confront them. Not only did she feel wounded by the children, but she felt betrayed and abandoned by her husband. She started to question why she was in this marriage and wondered if it had a chance of surviving. She wondered if she even *wanted* it to survive.

But Sandy decided to forgive her husband, try to understand his feelings, and talk with him about how his behavior affected her. Her husband agreed to go to counseling to help deal with their issues. Sandy and her husband both learned and grew from the experience. He realized it hurt his children and his wife for him to allow them to talk to her and treat her with disrespect. Surprising to him, but not to Sandy, when he started to correct their behavior, the children actually grew to respect him more. Sandy admired her husband's courage to confront the problem and take action to correct it. When he started coming to her defense, that endeared him even more to Sandy. Her love for her husband grew, and their marriage became stronger. It started with her decision to forgive.

Ashley's teenage stepson left a present for her to find after a weekend visit: dirty underwear with a load of "poo" in it, wadded up in the back of the dresser drawer—but not because he had an accident and was embarrassed. He had done it on purpose. Ashley decided to forgive her stepson even though he never apologized, never asked forgiveness, and never changed his attitude toward her. Ashley tried to discuss the issue with her husband, but he wanted nothing to do with it and insisted the issue was between Ashley and the teen. He refused to acknowledge that his son's behavior needed addressing and perhaps reflected a deeper issue. Unfortunately, the marriage did not survive. But Ashley decided to forgive her now ex-husband so she wouldn't be eaten alive by anger and bitterness. Even though the outcome wasn't what Ashley wanted, she speaks of her ex and his son without resentment and has gone on to live a fulfilling and rewarding life. It started with her decision to forgive.

Terry's stepdaughter, who lived full-time with Terry and her husband (the girl's biological father), left the day after high school graduation to go live with her biological mother in a different state, saying, "I've gotten everything I can get out of you." Her father had been granted full custody, and Terry had become her stepmother when she was still a preschooler. Terry had taught her everything she knew to teach a young girl and had even grown to love her. And this was what she got in return. But Terry decided to forgive. She forgave her stepdaughter for being ungrateful. She forgave her for breaking her heart. She forgave her for breaking her father's heart. She wished her stepdaughter no ill will and still prays for her and her biological mother. Terry is free from bitterness, and she no longer hurts when she thinks or speaks of the young woman. It started with the decision to forgive.

Kelsey's in-laws acted like human wrecking balls, criticizing her to her face, condemning her behind her back, and demeaning her in front of her stepchild. They undercut decisions her husband made and she supported regarding the child because they felt sorry for the "poor little thing" who had "been through so much." Still, Kelsey decided to forgive her in-laws. She also saw what being treated like a victim did to her stepchild, and she didn't like it. Neither did her husband.

Kelsey and her husband learned they couldn't make up for life's tough circumstances by depriving their child of necessary discipline.

Doing so only compounded the problem and made life harder for everyone. Kelsey also learned what God says about discipline:

> We have all had human fathers who disciplined us and we respected them for it. . . . Our fathers disciplined us for a little while as they thought best, but God disciplines us for our good, that we may share in his holiness. No discipline seems pleasant at the time, but painful. Later on, however, it produces a harvest of righteousness and peace for those who have been trained by it. (Hebrews 12:9, 10–11)

So Kelsey forgave her in-laws while maintaining the standards she and her husband deemed best for the child. Kelsey grew stronger in her own convictions as well and didn't allow what others thought to control her behavior. Her in-laws could see the fruitful results of her actions, and they grew to respect and even admire her. They also stopped critiquing her. Eventually Kelsey and her in-laws developed a close relationship that grew into love. It started with her decision to forgive.

(Speaking of in-laws, sometimes it may be necessary, as in Kelsey's case, not only to forgive but also to let them know that you cannot allow their interference in your family's business. Let them know that while you appreciate their concern, you will take steps to limit their negative influence. Mean it. Do it. By the way, this is best said by the person who is the direct relative, *not* the in-law.)

Karen's ex-husband lied to their youngest child and said that Karen had planned to abort him. In spite of her hurt and anger, Karen decided to forgive her ex. She also decided not to trash-talk her ex to her child. In time the child learned both the truth about the lie and the character of the one who told it. And the child loved and respected Karen all the more because of her actions. It started with Karen's decision to forgive.

God bless these stepmothers. God bless you. You may have suffered much worse than these stepmoms, but I'll bet you connect with
their stories. When we include our own worst-case scenarios, as well
as ten thousand lesser, yet still significant, offenses, we soon realize we
need help when it comes to forgiveness.

JESUS—RELATIONSHIP EXPERT

If we want wise advice, we go to our relationship expert. Jesus has been
dealing with hurting and hurtful people for a long time, and He knows
how best to handle our situations. He knows how to bring good out
of them. He knows how to heal our hearts. He will do that for us, and
He will let us participate with Him in the healing process.

We have been wounded and wronged by people in our own families, often intentionally. "I don't know how stepmoms make it," one
counselor commented. One of the best ways to stepparent successfully
is to practice forgiveness. We can forgive because we have been forgiven. It helps to remember that Jesus did the hard work of forgiveness
by dying on a cross. In His love and grace, Jesus invites us to receive His
forgiveness for our sins. After that, we are free to tap into that forgiveness and extend it to others.

Here's a simple but helpful illustration. We are like a pipe that's
open at both ends. Jesus pours His forgiveness into us, and as it flows
through us, it cleans away all our sludge and sticky mess. As forgiveness flows through us, we can direct it into the lives of others. We are
merely the vehicle through which Christ's forgiveness flows. We never
have to come up with forgiveness on our own. It's called forgiving by
faith—trusting Jesus to do the forgiving in and through us. And it's
freeing. What a kind Savior! How precious we must be to Him that He
would forgive us and enable us to forgive others as well.

If you have never asked Jesus to forgive your sins, this would be a good time to do so. He will free you of all guilt and condemnation and give you His very own righteousness (or goodness) in return, not because of anything you've done, but because He loves you, He is good, and He has the power, the authority, and the desire to do so. Please do it today. Jesus offers you a whole new life now (2 Corinthians 5:17), including the power to forgive.

"Forgiveness is essential. It's the first step in healing," Dr. James A. Graham tells us. "Forgiveness excuses me so that I can move on to experience healing. In Jesus Christ you are forgiven. Then you have the freedom to be healed.'

Forgiveness, healing, freedom. So lovely. So closely connected.

Yet even when we know we're forgiven, forgiveness can seem so hard. We cry, "If you only knew what they did to me!" We say that others don't deserve forgiveness. But once again, Jesus comes to our rescue. He has to, because . . .

- forgiveness doesn't come naturally to us.
- sometimes we need His help to even *want* to forgive.
- we're not sure what it means to forgive.
- we don't know how to forgive.
- we're not sure *we're* forgiven.

Sometimes we hesitate to forgive because we're afraid of what it means. See if this helps:

- Forgiveness never means what the other person did or said was okay.
- Forgiving doesn't nullify your suffering.
- Forgiveness doesn't mean you must trust the other person immediately, if ever.
- Forgiveness doesn't mean you must reconcile. Reconciliation isn't always healthy.

Before we make an important decision, it's wise to weigh the pros and cons. Here are a few of the pros of forgiveness:

1. Forgiveness is the key that opens the door to the cell where you have stayed locked up in bitterness, anger, and hatred.

2. Forgiveness means you can be free from thinking the same toxic thoughts over and over, which scientists now know can cause mental, emotional, and physical anguish, and can even affect your DNA.

3. Forgiveness frees you from the burden of trying to get even. It is casting your cares on God (1 Peter 5:7) and leaving them in His capable hands. He can deal with your offender and free you to get on with better, more productive endeavors in your life.

4. Forgiveness is the first step on your road to healing.

Here are the cons of forgiveness:

1.

2.

3.

That's right. There aren't any! You will never regret forgiving.

When You Don't Feel Like Forgiving

You may not feel like forgiving. And you may not feel better right away after you do. That's okay. Just like when you've been forgiven, you may not always *feel* forgiven. But when you decide to forgive, you are on your way to healing. I'm so proud of you!

Christian counselor and stepmom Jennifer Cecil understands the connection between forgiving and healing. She explains it to us this way: There's (1) our *position* and (2) our *condition*. Our position is totally cleansed and forgiven in Christ. Our condition, however, says that sometimes we don't always feel it. It takes us awhile to believe it. That's the healing process. In the same way, just because you face challenges in your feelings toward someone else along the way doesn't mean you haven't forgiven. Challenges will come.

You'll Be Reoffended

"In a stepfamily," Jennifer Cecil says, "you'll be reoffended. While you're working through one issue, here will come ten more." Her advice? "See it as a *condition*, not a problem. A problem can disappear through finding and applying a solution. A condition must be managed over time."

Keep on forgiving. Every day, if necessary. Over and over. The same people for the same things. "Seventy-seven times," Jesus said in Matthew 18:22.

If you struggle with thinking, *It will take me a long time to forgive this*, think again. The decision to forgive—and forgiveness itself—can happen in a heartbeat.

Healing Takes Time

The decision to forgive can happen in a heartbeat, but people *heal* at different rates. According to Jennifer Cecil, temperament, past trauma, and the severity of the offense all affect the speed of recovery, but it doesn't matter how long healing takes. Either way it's miraculous.

Cecil outlined for us a step-by-step process for healing.

1. *Healing begins with the all-important decision to forgive.*

2. *As an observer, explore what's in your soul.* Be aware of your thoughts. What are your feelings? Ask yourself, "What triggers me? What reminds me of what this person did to me?" Be honest. Write it down.

But Cecil cautions, "Don't pray for God to take away the feelings. Feelings are like an indicator light in our car. They show if something's not working. What we really need is to pull over and check what's wrong, not just smash [the indicator light]."

Christian counselors Dallas and Nancy Demmitt, authors of *Can You Hear Me Now?* agree on how important it is to be aware of what we're thinking:

> We ask people to begin writing down the thoughts they are constantly hearing in their minds that result in fear, anger, sadness, shame, and conflict with others. Why? Because these are often the thoughts that contradict what God says. . . . We also ask them to write down the truth—what Scripture says in light of their new identity in Christ, in contrast to what they have been hearing.[2]

Keep reminding yourself of truth.

3. *Invite someone in.* Cecil recommends a trusted, nonjudgmental Christian friend. Let your friend know what's going on with you. Bring the issue into the light. Healing can unfold as you work through your thoughts and feelings.

Cecil has seen this in her practice. "There can be miraculous healing simply through sharing. There is power in transparency," she says. "You unburden your soul." And sometimes that's all it takes. "God lifts the burden from your soul. It's no longer there. It's gone."

Cecil advises, "Work things through with the purpose of sharing to be free, so you are not stuck. We don't just 'nurse and rehearse' our offense. There's no life in that. There's death." She adds, "If you've had lots of trauma, you may need professional help. If you're stuck, see somebody."

4. *Most important, Cecil counsels, "Invite Jesus to join you in your feelings.* Say something like, 'Lord, I trust You enough to invite You into the yuck. Come and join me in my feelings so that I am not alone.' He is acquainted with grief. He knows the feeling. Let Him sit with you in it. A lot of times that is healing in itself."

Jennifer Cecil points out that "God is interested in our peace. When we work through and settle things in our souls, we will have peace. God will bring it to pass. He will complete it. Whatever distresses your soul, process it and bring it back to God. It takes as long as it takes, so settle in and relax. We have to *fight* for our *peace*," Cecil concludes with a smile.

And we *can* rest knowing that we have been—and are—forgiven.

Finding It Hard to Forgive?

Having trouble forgiving? I know it can seem difficult, if not impossible, but see if any of the following advice helps:

- Don't wait to forgive until the person who offended you repents and asks for forgiveness. That may never happen. You know people right now who fall into this category. In fact, some of them may be dead and incapable of asking. Go ahead and forgive if the person's actions still upset you. Take the initiative. Remember, God is an expert at forgiving people, and He will enable *you* to do it.

- Every time you need to forgive someone, remind yourself how fully and completely God has forgiven you, even for being unforgiving. Ask Him to forgive through you. And He will. Every time.

- Stay focused on God's forgiveness of *you*, not only your sin. Your sin's been taken care of; it's gone. God says He remembers it no more (Isaiah 43:25). He wants us to remember our forgiveness. Jesus even instituted communion for us to remember not our sin but *Him* and His forgiveness (Luke 22:19). Jesus said those who have been forgiven much, love much (7:47). We have all been forgiven much—much more than we know. And when we love Him much, we love

others. "We love because he first loved us" (1 John 4:19).
When we love Jesus, we love others; when we love others, we
forgive them.

- When feelings of forgiveness just aren't there, look to the
cross and say, "There's the forgiveness. There's the forgiveness
for me and the forgiveness He allows me to pass on to others.
He honors me by letting me partner with Him in forgiving the world." That's part of the meaning of "taking every
thought captive to the obedience of Christ" (2 Corinthians
10:5, NASB). His obedience of dying on a cross empowers us
to live freely. We are transformed as we behold Him.

- Don't get distracted from forgiving by the realization that
someone doesn't deserve forgiveness. That's a given. You're
right; they don't deserve it. None of us deserve grace and
forgiveness. *Grace*, defined as "undeserved, unmerited favor,"
is a gift.

JESUS HUGS ME—AND YOU

During a time in my life when I was having trouble forgiving, the following scenario helped me get to a point where I even *liked* the idea of
forgiving. See how it affects you.

Imagine Jesus standing right beside you reassuring you of His
love, one arm around your shoulder and a hand where you
can see the nail scar. His glory surrounds you, and His beauty
indwells you. His Spirit of love, grace, forgiveness, and joy fills
you with peace. Your heart is so full of love and gratitude to
Him for His love and grace that you no longer want anything
less than His grace to fill your heart. You are partnering with

Jesus in His mission to save the world, forgiving each person who has offended you, one at a time.

In her book *Wounded by God's People: Discovering How God's Love Heals Our Hearts*, Anne Graham Lotz writes,

I have been asked repeatedly, 'Anne, how have you experienced healing of your wounds? How have you been able to move past them?' The answer, which may seem simplistic but is the one that works, is that the healing antidote to wounds is forgiveness. But I don't stop with just the decision to forgive. Once I have made the decision to forgive, I move forward by doing something for the person who has hurt me. . . . I need to do something for the person I am forgiving. Something I would do for no other reason than it's my act of worship—worship of One who laid down His life for me as His own act of sacrificial, loving forgiveness.[3]

My response? "Anne, you inspire me. That's great advice. I'm going to start doing the same thing. Thank you."

WHEN YOU ARE THE ONE
WHO NEEDS FORGIVING

That awkward moment when . . . well, let's face it, stepfamily life is full of awkward moments. Be ready so that when they happen, you won't take them too personally or too seriously. As much as you can, go with the flow and have as much fun with them as you can. Awkward can be bonding—and fun, at least eventually. But awkward moments can also be cause for forgiveness.

Like the time Abby's middle school promoted the idea of students wearing Valentine's-themed clothing to celebrate the day. I wanted Abby to participate, and since she didn't own anything along those lines, I went out the day before to buy something for her. I couldn't find a thing and began to panic. In the rush, I spotted a T-shirt with an endearing Valentine's message. *Perfect,* I thought. *That's sweet.* I showed it to Abby when she got home from school, and she loved it.

Only after she left for school the next day did I suffer an attack of the spinners—where something you've said or done hits you with such force that it spins you right out of your chair or bed or wherever you happen to be. While cute at first glance, that T-shirt carried a sexual innuendo that, in my haste, I had missed. (Trust me, it was very inappropriate. I'm too embarrassed to write it here!) The meaning of the innuendo hit me, and I died a thousand deaths until Abby returned home from school and I could see how her day went. *Will anybody else catch it?* I wondered. Just how savvy were all those other prepubescents?

Apparently, very. Abby was mortified. I was embarrassed and so, so sorry. I would never have bought her something like that *if only I had realized.* She forgave me, thankfully. But guess what? Just last Valentine's Day (twenty-five years later), a "friend" on Facebook reminded her of that T-shirt and added that her mom couldn't believe some mother would do that to her child! Who would do such a thing? *Some wicked stepmother?*

It was an honest mistake born of a desire to help my child fit in, but I blew it that time. We all make mistakes, stepmom.

These eight words will serve you well: "I'm sorry. I was wrong. Please forgive me." No justifying, no defending, no implicating the other person as the cause of our offense or contributing to our actions. We own our fault, and we own our sorrow because of it.

ASKING FORGIVENESS WHEN WE NEED TO

I know I have done and said things that have hurt my children, like the two examples of thoughtlessness I've already mentioned. I hate that. My children and stepchildren haven't had the advantage of having a perfect mother/stepmother. I'm sure I have contributed to every issue they face. No matter that it's not even possible, I have wanted to be perfect for them.

So in addition to asking forgiveness for individual offenses as I've committed them, I have said to each one of my adult children individually something like this (and Jim and I together have said it to them as well):

> We are so sorry we couldn't be the perfect parents you deserve.
> We know we've done stupid things that have hurt you and not
> helped you. We haven't done them on purpose. But we know
> we have lost our tempers, we've misjudged you, and we've
> focused on the wrong things at times and left important issues
> unaddressed. You have issues to deal with because of us. We're
> sorry for any way we have messed you up, and we ask you
> to please forgive us. We've always had the best of intentions
> toward you, but our actions haven't always reflected it. We love
> you very much, and we think that in spite of us, you've turned
> out pretty great, and we are so proud of you.

And you know what? It has drawn us closer to our kids. They have appreciated the gesture, have been quick to forgive, and have even responded with gracious comments of their own. But even if they hadn't, it was still the right thing for Jim and me to do.

At an appropriate time, try apologizing for your shortcomings and watch what happens. If you're at the beginning of your stepmother journey, you can tell your stepchildren that you wish you could be a perfect stepmother for them, but you know you can't. Reassure them of your good intentions and tell them you know you're going to need a lot of forgiveness, and that you plan to forgive them when they need it as well.

If you've got a few years under your belt as a stepmother, you can tell your stepchildren you're sorry for all the times you have failed them, you don't mean to make life more difficult for them, and you appreciate the people they are and are in the process of becoming. You may have done and said things you didn't even realize at the time were offensive or hurtful. This can help heal those wounds. What a gift to give your stepkids! In addition to being gracious, it's disarming and helps allay any hostility toward you.

Even if you don't get the response you want right away, or ever, you know you have done the right thing and modeled forgiveness for your stepchildren. Believe me, they will remember it. I know of other stepmothers who have done this, and they have also seen the benefits.

Of course, once you have asked for forgiveness, it opens the door for the offended to grow in grace and offer you forgiveness. But what if you ask someone for forgiveness, and he or she doesn't or won't forgive you? Then it's no longer your problem. You've done your part. It's now between them and God. Once again, you are free.

What about those times we shock even ourselves by the way we act?

- What if you have demeaned or degraded your stepchildren, intentionally abusing them mentally, physically, spiritually, emotionally, or verbally?
- What if you have never said one encouraging, edifying, or uplifting word to your stepchildren?

- What if you have criticized or lied about your stepchildren's biological mom to get them to like you, or to deliberately hurt them?
- What if you have sabotaged your husband's efforts to have one-on-one time with his children because you are jealous of the time and attention he gives them?
- What if you have harbored anger, bitterness, and unforgiveness in your heart toward your stepchildren and haven't taken steps to change?

Even if this describes you, even if you think of yourself as a wicked stepmother, there is good news for you. What you're doing now or have done in the past doesn't define you. You can be forgiven and renewed, free of guilt, shame, and condemnation. Who hasn't lost her temper, said things she regretted, left kind and thoughtful actions undone, and behaved in a hurtful and disrespectful manner? I can't think of a single soul. Everyone is acceptable, lovable, and redeemable in God's eyes—and His are the eyes that see truth. So remember, it's not about how wicked a stepmother you are; it's about how wonderful a Savior He is. Bring your "wicked" ways to the cross and watch Him forgive them.

Consider this encouraging thought from author and youth pastor Kevin Huggins: "He [God] never gives them [parents] the power to destroy their kids' lives. Parents, even at their worst, do not have the power to rob their kids of the capacity to develop into loving, mature adults."[4]

A marriage, family, and child therapist shared this thought:

How our kids develop is not totally and completely in our hands. As they grow, our kids must take responsibility for their actions and their choices. They are not the total product of our mistakes, nor are they the total product of our successes. Rather, our kids are more a product of how they choose to respond to both our successes and our failures.[5]

Do I hear a sigh of relief?

No More Stepmom Guilt

Dr. Chip Moody, professor of pastoral ministry at Phoenix Seminary, shared these observations with us:

> As a pastor, I have listened to hundreds of moms confessing their mom-guilt, as though being a mom should somehow make a woman omniscient when it comes to every need of this alien stranger she is raising. And if mom is a *stepmom*, you triple the sense of self-loathing. She feels as though every mistake is counted and no grace afforded. Bad enough that stepmoms question every move they make; it's worse that they do not enjoy the grace of God in their parenting. Hanging on to past mistakes is a trap with no way out, a maze with no exit. The apostle Paul wrote, "But one thing I do: forgetting what lies behind and reaching forward to what lies ahead, I press on toward the goal for the prize of the upward call of God in Christ Jesus" (Philippians 3:13–14, NASB). Yesterday is gone and covered in grace. Every victim of stepmom-guilt needs to learn the freedom of *forgetting the past and looking forward.*

Dr. Moody concluded with this advice: "When thoughts of past poor decisions or life choices creep in, don't ruminate! Instead ask God to give you *clarity* about what kind of good decisions you can make today."

Counselor Jennifer Cecil advises all of us who are stepmoms to "think of *one thing* to change. Ask God to empower you. Don't be overwhelmed or paralyzed. You don't need to overhaul your whole personality at once. God will honor your decision, and He will help you."

Do you still struggle with feelings of guilt even though you know you are forgiven? Let's change that today. You've suffered with guilt long enough. Focus on receiving God's grace for you and stop beating yourself up. Jesus took the beating for you. Our part is to receive the grace and rest in it. To borrow a line from one of my favorite movies, guilt "is like [a] television set on a honeymoon—unnecessary!"[6]

In my research, I discovered that most stepmothers are quicker to grant forgiveness to others than to accept it for themselves. Tired of trying to forgive yourself? Of course you are. It's a backbreaking, wearisome burden. So please, quit trying. You may be surprised to learn that forgiving yourself isn't necessary.

Jodi Werhanowicz, Christian counselor, speaker, stepmom, and author of Mary Kay Beard's biography *Rogue Angel: The Spiritual Journey of One of the FBI's Ten Most Wanted*, says, "If we could forgive ourselves, why would we need Jesus? What we are really saying is that His work on the cross is not sufficient. The idea that our own forgiveness is what will truly set us free is just another way the enemy tries to take our focus off Jesus and put it back on ourselves."[7]

Suzanne Eller says it this way in *The Unburdened Heart*: "Go as deep into Scripture as you want and you will not find where you or I have the ability to forgive ourselves. . . . Shift the focus to total receptivity of His grace. It's a gift that you not only receive, but you give. As you receive it, you are able to pour it out on others."[8]

Jesus forgives you and saves you from the burden of having to forgive yourself. He didn't come to condemn you; He came to save you. And He does good work.

No matter how many times you've heard it, that's still astonishingly good news.

One stepmom said, "It helped me be able to quit making this about what *I* had to do and how hard it is to do it. I do not discount my deep wounds, my betrayal, my anguish. I feel the pain, I own the suffering, and then I take my attention off myself, how badly I have been hurt, how horrible the people are who have hurt me, and put my attention on Jesus and His finished work on the cross. He did the dying. He does the forgiving. I receive the blessing, which includes being empowered to forgive others and to be healed myself. I'm free and I'm healed."

What a positive, encouraging, and happy ending to any offense.

After you have forgiven the one who hurt you and worked through the steps to healing, remember these three counselor-recommended strategies:

1. I will not keep bringing up the offense to *myself*.
2. I will not keep bringing up the offense to *the one who hurt me.*
3. I will not keep bringing up the offense to *others.*

Forgiven people forgive people. Loved people love people. You are both. This is who you are, child of God. Beloved and forgiven. Empowered to love and forgive others. It's one of the benefits of being His daughter. God has given us amazing grace, and we can do amazing things through His grace—like forgive and receive forgiveness. It's part of our Great Adventure.

Stepmoms are some of the best forgivers I know. The stepmoms I told you about earlier all chose to forgive. They are also some of the happiest stepmoms I know. Even though their circumstances weren't all they had hoped they would be, they experienced joy because they chose to forgive. The most contented stepmoms make the decision to forgive any offenses, and quickly. They decide to live in Forgiveness Town. That's right. They make it their new address, and so can you.

Those stepmoms have great stories of forgiveness. But I haven't told you the best story yet. Would you like to hear it? Well, you'll have to tell it to me, because the best story is *yours*. It's about *you* and *your experience* with the love and grace of Jesus. There's nothing better. Be assured, you have a great story to tell, and I would love to hear it.

PRAYER

Dear Lord, help me accept the obvious—that an imperfect human cannot be a perfect stepmom—and instead remind me often that You are raising my stepchild with me.

THIRTEEN

"What My Stepmom Did Right"

Delight yourself in the LORD and he will

give you the desires of your heart.

—PSALM 37:4

Kathi and Carol

Since Carol and I (Kathi) started writing this book, we've come across a lot of discouraging facts and stories about the state of blended families. And when I asked stepmoms what they did right with their stepkids? Well, let's just say the responses were a little less than encouraging. But when I asked stepkids if they could share with me what their stepmom did right, the floodgates opened up.

Interesting, right?

Sure, there were a couple of stepkids who started off with "No, but I can sure tell you everything she did wrong." But the overwhelming majority wanted to tell me what their stepmoms did to bless them.

The day after I asked my friends on Facebook what stepmoms did right, I had dinner with a group of MOPS (Mothers of Preschoolers) leaders in Hanford, California. One of those leaders was Jodie Bissig, a stepkid herself. We had a long talk at the dinner table about the impact her stepmom had on her life. I asked Jodie if she could talk about how, as an adult, she now sees her stepmother's influence in her life when she was a child. Here's what she told me:

My stepmom was great because she made me feel like she really loved me. Not the idea of me, not just because she loved my dad, and not because she was "supposed to." She made me feel loved and accepted just for being me. She didn't ever make me feel like she was trying to be anything other than another supportive, loving adult in my life. It took the pressure off of our relationship. It didn't need to "be" anything; we could just be the two of us, independent from all the other relationships in our lives.

She never, ever, ever spoke poorly about my mother (although she easily could have; there's plenty to say!). My stepmom has always understood that while I have a complicated, messy relationship with my birth mother, it would have been inappropriate for her to share her opinion with me about it. And truly, there would have been no way for her to win. If she had agreed with me that my birth mother is crazy, she would have been insulting someone I am biologically made from. If she had tried to defend my mother, she would have risked making me feel as if my feelings weren't valid.

I would tell any stepparent, no matter the circumstances, to try to stay very neutral about any issues with the biological parent. The child is 50 percent of that person, good or bad. If you insult or criticize a birth parent in any way, it's very easy for children to see that negative trait in themselves.

And last is perhaps the thing I value most about my stepmom. The best gift she has given me is to stay so in love with my dad. She takes such great care of him, and they are very happy together. As a child of divorce, I cannot express how much of a relief it is to see my dad's happiness. He is loved, and she makes him happy. That's the best gift a stepparent can give their stepchild.

I wanted to share what Jodie had to say because I think there are three things she talked about that are so doable for us as stepmoms in connecting with our stepkids:

1. *Her stepmom valued her on her own.* Yes, we enter into these relationships because of our stepkids' dads, but our stepkids want to know that they are valued for the people they are, not just because they are connected to their fathers.

2. *Her stepmom remained neutral when it came to her biological mom.* Something I've seen with all these stepkids is that eventually they start to see their parents for who they truly are—the good, the bad, and the ugly. They don't need us to point it out to them. One of my mentors in stepparenting told me early on, "Just report the facts. Don't editorialize. When their mom at the last minute can't pick them up from school, just say, 'Your mom couldn't make it, so she asked me to come,' not, 'Yep, your flaky mom decided she was too busy to pick you up today, so I had to leave work to do it.' While it may be the truth (or at least may feel that way to you), it doesn't help your stepchild's relationship with his or her mom or you."

3. *Her stepmom cared for her dad.* Kids from divorced families are often saddled with an additional burden besides the pain of their parents splitting up. They now must worry about who is going to "take care" of the unmarried parent. Who will love them, make sure they are eating healthy and seeing the doctor, and so forth? What a gift to our stepkids to let them know that their dad is our priority. They don't have to take on the additional responsibility of being the bottom line for their dad. As Jodie said, the best gift you can give your stepkids is to take care of and love their dad.

In addition to Jodie's story, I received dozens of other odes to stepmoms. I thought it would be helpful to see what these adult stepkids valued in their relationships with their stepmoms, and what we can learn from them. Keep reading!

"SHE WAS NOT A MOM AND NOT MY BEST FRIEND, BUT A MENTOR"

Jessica told us,

> My stepmom didn't try to be my mom, and she didn't try to be my best friend. But she was and is my mentor. She was the person who provided guidance that I needed when it felt like the world around me was caving in. She focused on me when she could have easily gotten caught up in the drama that is divorce. God put her in my life at the exact moment I needed her, and she has been a blessing to me ever since.

Over and over, grown stepkids talked about the unique roles their stepmoms played in their lives. One woman described it as "that aunt you really, really like, but she lives with you all the time."

For most kids, it wasn't an instant connection. It took time to develop the roles that everyone was going to play and how they were going to play them. But it was heartening to see that even those relationships that started off with a lot of drama and angst turned out to be some of the best relationships these kids have had in their lives.

The Truths We Should Take Away from This

- If you're just starting your stepmom journey or are somewhere in the middle of it, time is on your side. There is still time for God to work a miracle in your relationship with your stepchild.

- Most kids aren't looking for another mom. We need to have relationships with our steps that are different from any other they have in their lives. We're in a parental role, but in most cases, not mom or dad. It's this third, unnamed role that our stepkids need.
- The reason this child now has you as a stepmom is because he or she has been through some kind of struggle—a death, a divorce, or an abandonment. While your stepchild's biological parents may be in the midst of drama, you can be the one to be neutral when it comes to the parents' issues and just be there for that child.

"She Helped Me Have a Relationship with My Dad"

Jacy shared,

> My stepmom made it possible for me to have a relationship with my father, whom I didn't meet until I was seventeen. She really helped bridge the communication gap (he had no idea how to talk to a daughter) and smooth out the rough spots as we found our way.

As I'm writing this, Roger and I are at a cabin in the woods with limited cell-phone coverage. Roger got a text from his daughter Amanda, letting him know that her car was in need of four thousand dollars' worth of repairs. Roger texted her back, but we have no way of knowing whether she received the text. We have a way to make phone calls, but it's over our computer, and it's clumsy and hard to hear. I encouraged Roger to call her anyway. Yes, she may have received the text, and she and her boyfriend may be handling it, but I told Roger,

"When a girl is overwhelmed and calls her dad, she needs to talk to her dad."

I may not do everything right in this stepmom journey, but I am laser focused when it comes to my husband having a great, connected relationship with his kids. He and his son take off for a couple of days every year to watch meteors, and sometimes he and his daughter will go to lunch, dinner, or even Disneyland together. (Don't feel sorry for me. I've married into a family that can't get enough Disney. Trust me, I've had my fill.)

I don't see my husband's time away with his kids as anything but an investment in their lives and our relationship. When he and his kids are at peace, it builds every connection my husband has—with his kids and with me.

The Truths We Should Take Away from This

- As stepmoms, so much of how our stepkids view us is through the relationship they have with their dads.
- By encouraging a healthy relationship between your stepchild and his or her dad, you are building all the relationships in your blended family.
- A lot of this stepmom stuff is not entirely up to you. Be proactive and talk to your husband about how to make your relationship better with his kids by his being connected to his kids.

"She Honored My Mom"

Sherry recalled this special memory of her stepmom:

My first mom (and oldest brother) died in a car accident when I was twelve. My dad remarried just over a year later, and my

second mom is just as wonderful as my first. None of us think
of her as our stepmom; she's simply our mom. One thing she
did was to make sure that nothing changed in our relationships
with our first mom's family.

I'm sure it wasn't easy feeling like she was being compared to
our first mom, but she immersed herself in that side of the family, and I am so proud of her for that. The other thing that really
stood out was how she honored my first mom at my wedding. I
forget how she put it, but in her "parental speech" she acknowledged what a huge role my first mom played in raising me to
become the woman I was. It was very touching. My siblings and
I feel so blessed to have had two amazing moms, not just one.

Every stepmom has a different relationship with her stepkids'
mom. Maybe Mom is present in her kids' lives, maybe she has abandoned them, or as in Carol's case, maybe Mom has passed away. This
is where we need to be totally unselfish in getting our needs met and
be ready to fill the role that our stepchild needs us to play.

Kelly shares a very practical way that her stepmom honored both
Kelly and her mother: "Whenever my stepmom came across what she
thought would be a treasured family item, she would ask one of us if
we wanted it. For example, she noticed I didn't have crystal, so she gave
me my mom's set."

The Truths We Should Take Away from This

- We need to stamp out any insecurities about being compared to the first mom. God has a role in our stepchildren's
  lives that we are designed to play. We need to play it to the
  best of our ability.
- Part of honoring your stepchildren's first mom is making sure, to the best of your ability, that the kids continue

to have a relationship with their mom's family. If she isn't actively mothering your stepkids (because of death, abandonment, illness, etc.), then be the one who makes sure that phone calls are made and cards are sent. I know this can be hard, especially if your stepkids' mom has disappointed you and your stepkids, but this isn't for her (mostly); it's for them.

- Let your stepchildren figure out the roles. Sherry ended up calling her stepmom "Mom"—that was right for her. My stepkids call me their stepmom or Kathi, and when referring to Roger and me, they say, "My dad and stepmom"; or if someone understands the situation, they may just refer to us as "my parents." Either way is perfectly fine with me. They have a mom, and that title is for her.

"She Let Our Relationship Go at My Pace"

Janelle had this to say about her stepmom:

> My stepmom never pushed to be my "mom" or tried to take the place of her, but she also never gave up on me, and she supported me like a mother should. She wasn't pushy about getting me to like her at first, which was refreshing. She wanted me to want to come to her with things naturally. And it worked, because now that I am older, I am probably closer to her than most people.

Sometimes it feels like we're making no headway in this blessing called stepparenting. The stepkids remind us on a daily basis that we are not, in fact, their real moms (even though they still need to be picked up from soccer practice and want to know if we washed their uniforms yet). But even when we don't see progress, sometimes it's happening in sure, small ways that go without notice. And who knows, maybe that kid who pushed you away for all those years will turn out to be one of your biggest fans as an adult:

The Truths We Should Take Away from This

- God is working even when we don't see the results.
- You can demand respectful behavior, but you can never demand a relationship.
- The timing is up to your stepchild and God.

"She Pointed Me Toward Jesus"

Sherry's stepmom passed on the greatest legacy of all:

> My stepmom was a true gift from the Lord. She prayed for my sister and me to come to know Jesus. She was the one who took me to church and was there when I accepted Christ. She was the one who taught me what it was to be a Christian woman, even when my dad wasn't serving the Lord (at the time). She taught me to cook and to bake (all from scratch!). I watched her be a true hostess, serving others, and I learned from the best. She has a sweet spirit, and she loved us like we were her own. But most of all, she was there for my mom while my mom battled cancer. My stepmom and my dad prayed for her, and my stepmom would send my mom cards with prayers and encouragement. True gifts.

Depending on the family your stepchild grew up in, you may be the only influence on that child when it comes to Christ. To see your stepchildren's God-given talents, to recognize your stepchildren as the unique creations they are, and then to love them with the love of Christ (even when they may not be acting very "lovable") is an amazing gift to give to our stepkids.

The Truths We Should Take Away from This

- Your stepkids may not appreciate your faith at the moment, but there may be a day that they do. I know that it means something to my stepkids when I let them know that their dad and I are praying for them. We also pray for their friends, their school situations, and their jobs. The more time you spend praying for your stepchildren, the harder it is to judge them. I know that prayer has been a huge factor in why I am now close to my stepkids.

- We can pray unselfishly for our stepkids. I pray every day that my stepkids would become more of what God wants them to be. I get to pray for them in big and bold ways. When Roger is fretting about some decision they've made, I can skip the worrying (which I never seem to skip with my own two kids) and go straight to prayer and hope.

"SHE TREATS MY KIDS LIKE HER OWN GRANDKIDS"

Kelly shares another way that her stepmom blessed not just her but her child as well:

> She treated my daughter just like all her other grandchildren and even chastised them for thinking my daughter was any different. Because of this, my daughter had the benefit of a loving grandma and cousins she loves.

This one totally surprised me because I've spent so much time thinking about building my relationship with my stepkids that I never thought about when they have kids. But they will. And I know I will love those babies as much as I love my own kids' babies.

The Truths We Should Take Away from This

- One of the greatest gifts we can give our stepkids is to love who they love. This is the deepest kind of acceptance we can communicate to them.
- Everyone needs to be reminded that they are inherently valued, no matter what their path into the family is.

WHAT MY OWN STEPKIDS THOUGHT
I DID RIGHT

After I thought I was done writing this chapter, I had a friend read it over. Her question? "So did you ask your stepkids what you did right?"

Gulp.

So I did one of the bravest things a stepmom could do: I called my stepkids and asked them what I'd done right.

Double gulp.

Here is the biggest blessing from this book for me. Amanda said,

One of the things that made this whole stepfamily thing so much easier is that you always told me the truth, even when it was hard, even when I didn't like what was going on. You always were open with me and let me ask you questions. I remember you taking me out to coffee just to let me tell you how I felt, and you didn't try to correct me or convince me; you just let me talk, and you listened.

Jeremy said,

You always supported me, especially with sports. You always
took me to hockey and track practice and showed up for my
meets and games. You were interested in the things I was doing,
and that meant a lot to me.

Now that Amanda and Jeremy are twenty-six and twenty-four,
respectively, my relationships with them are completely different from
when I was going to hockey meets and trying to make these fractions
of a family pull together. But what they remember most are not those
times when I often felt like the biggest failure; they remember me
showing up and staying present in their lives.

Now *that* is a gift.

SPECIAL MEMORIES OF
GOD'S FAITHFULNESS

Fast-forward thirty years from the Halloween bonding experience I
(Carol) had with Abby. I'm sitting in a Cheesecake Factory restaurant
opening Mother's Day gifts, but what I really see is God's faithfulness
in answering thirty years of prayers. One gift in particular needs men-
tioning: a hand-crafted memory book Abby gave me, which is filled
with handwritten cards of special memories she enjoys of the two of
us. Come read along with me:

- "I remember our first Easter together. You took me to buy a
  new, white dress with blue satin ribbons. I also got a matching white hat, white tights, and white shoes. I was so happy."
  (Note: I love how completely she forgives and didn't even
  mention the Easter Bunny fiasco part of this day. Thank you,
  Abby!)

- "You humored me the day I wanted to lip-sync an entire Amy Grant album, and for the entire neighborhood, at that! You helped me make flyers, and you even made brownies to serve as refreshments. Granny Jane was the only one who showed!"
- "One day in the car, when I was in second grade, I told you I wanted to be cool. You asked me what that meant. I told you it meant wearing fluorescent colors and jelly sandals. When I got home from school, you had bought me jelly shoes and some fluorescent clothes. What an awesome mom you are!" (Note: We also discussed that there is more to being cool than the clothes you wear, so this wouldn't always be the proper response. But sometimes you just need the jellies.)
- "You always encouraged me to spend time with my biological mother's family. You also let me know it was okay to remember my mother, Cathy."
- "You made me my first photo album of pictures just of me. It was the first time I saw pictures of me as an infant. I will never forget that and will forever be grateful."

Abby remembered more experiences, some of which we've already talked about. But I chose ones from the early years to show how planting seeds can reap a bountiful harvest over time. And the common theme running through them all? Expressing to her that I thought about her, cared about her, and then took the time to show her. That's what love looks like. My hunch, stepmom, is that you are doing an even better job than you think.

THE THREE BIG TRUTHS WE NEED TO UNDERSTAND AND LIVE EVERY DAY

1. *Our stepkids think we did a better job than we thought we did at the time.* Remember how I (Kathi) asked stepmoms what they did right

and got almost no responses? But then I asked the stepkids what their stepmoms did right and got a load of responses? How is it that none of us can point to anything we did right? And did you notice that a lot of what the adult kids appreciated was when their stepmoms stayed neutral? Again, no rewards are handed out for biting our tongues until they bleed, but that's often what our stepkids appreciate most.

So many of the notes I received started with the idea of "Now that I'm an adult, I can appreciate all that my stepmom did for us as a family."

2. *With stepparenting, the rewards come later.* Another idea that came across a lot in the messages I got from stepkids was, "Now that I'm older, I have a great relationship with my stepmom." Because when we're in the midst of it, there are very few rewards for stepmoms.

Rarely do younger kids or teens throw their arms around you and squeal, "You're the best stepmommy ever!" Yeah . . . that just doesn't happen. No one is handing out blue ribbons for getting lunches made every day or preparing healthy meals for the family.

But as adults (especially starting when the stepchild moves out of the house), stepkids and parents often forge new relationships with each other.

3. *Time is on your side.* If I could give every stepmom one piece of practical advice on all this stepstuff, it would be this: For stepmoms, a lot of the hard issues don't need to be resolved; they just need to be endured.

We don't want to raise bratty, entitled, or disrespectful kids or stepkids, so our natural inclination is to make sure we stay on top of everything and clamp down hard when our kids aren't doing what they are supposed to. In the first several years of Roger's and my marriage, my stepson, Jeremy, was rarely outright disrespectful (that's just not his personality), but he would be moody, irritable, and just plain lousy to get along with. Amanda, my stepdaughter, spent the first year of our being a family making sure that we knew how much our marriage was ruining her life. She would try to make Roger feel guilty about it, and then her mom would call Roger to reinforce how much it was making Amanda's life miserable.

On top of that, my own kids were having a hard time adjusting to the new situation and were acting out in ways that threatened to drive a wedge between Roger and me. Throw in an ex-wife who called once a week to let us know what we were doing wrong, and my ex-husband who was whispering some not-so-kind words about me in my kids' ears, and the whole situation just felt completely overwhelming.

Do you know how many of the above-mentioned issues are a problem today?

None.

Not one.

Yes, some of this is because we got some wise counsel on how to handle those circumstances, but for the most part, the biggest factor in getting them resolved? Time.

Jeremy grew up. He and I had a great talk one day where he admitted that he had been angry with me because if I hadn't married his dad, he thought his parents might have gotten back together. (Even though they had been divorced for more than ten years.) Eventually Jeremy's relationship with his dad changed. While they still act like father and son, they also have a more adult relationship that has allowed space for me.

Amanda matured into the beautiful young woman she is today, but not because we had a long talk or imposed a set of guidelines on how to behave. She was already a pretty great girl in a tough situation. (When your dad marries a new woman, and she has two kids who are now your stepbrother and stepsister for life, it's a tough situation.) Once Amanda got her bearings and a little growth under her belt, she found her footing, and now we love being together.

My stepkids' mom and my ex-husband naturally became less involved as the kids got older. Now we only need to communicate with her about big, important stuff, not the minutiae of everyday life that can just wear a mother down.

Eventually my own kids evened out as well. Yes, some of it was parenting, but some of it was just waiting for them to grow up a little bit (and a bit of me and Roger growing up as well).

Often, issues seem like life or death when you're in the midst of the problem, but sooner or later you start to develop a sense of which issues you need to deal with as a couple, and which issues you need to wait out. That's when this blended-family thing becomes so much easier. It'll happen, stepmom. Hold on. Keep trusting. Keep praying. Keep loving.

Hope for the Long Haul

I (Kathi) hope that the words and insights in this chapter brought you some hope. You may not be in the "reward" part of stepparenting, but for so many of us, there *is* a reward that will eventually come—whether it's having a great adult relationship with your stepchild, being the prayer warrior who is standing in the gap for your stepkid, or knowing that you had the best influence you could under difficult circumstances. For so many of us, that reward is going to come later.

As a mom and a stepmom, I sometimes take the short view of parenting. When kids aren't picking up their clothes, or they've decided to use the kitchen counter as a storage device for their gym shoes, I tend to, well, lose my mind. But one of the gifts my husband brings to our stepparenting adventures is the long view. He doesn't think that every missed baseball practice is the end of the world. He can reprimand a kid for a missed curfew, and his mind doesn't immediately go to that child's future as a vagrant or con artist. He's really great that way.

My favorite passage of Scripture is Romans 12:10–12 (NKJV):

Be kindly affectionate to one another with brotherly love, in
honor giving preference to one another; not lagging in diligence, fervent in spirit, serving the Lord; rejoicing in hope,
patient in tribulation, continuing steadfastly in prayer.

Those last three charges are the ones I cling to:

1. *Rejoicing in hope.* Hope is a beautiful thing. Hope gets us
   out of bed in the morning. Hope gets us to see beyond the
   grunts and moans of our kids and move to the place of what
   God can do in our lives.
2. *Patient in tribulation.* Patience is the hardest thing in my life
   to ask for (I'm terrified anytime I pray for it). But as a stepmom, I need it more than any other human being I know.
   It takes a long time for us to figure out our roles (and even
   longer for our stepkids sometimes).
3. *Steadfast in prayer.* Prayer gets us through the times when
   we feel like running away from home and changing the
   locks.

Carol and I want you to know that we believe in you. You've chosen
a thorny path, but it's also the one with the crazy, Willy Wonka–like
flowers strewn along the way. Your forever after is going to be beautiful. Stepmom, you've got this. God has given you everything you need
to take the long view of stepparenting. And while your stepchild may
never rise up and call you blessed (though he or she might eventually!),
years from now you may get a "Yeah, my stepmom is pretty cool."

Take it. And rejoice.

I (Carol) also want to remind you that your success as a stepmom
doesn't depend on the current status of your relationship with your
stepkids. Focus on building into their lives; don't focus on the outcome,

because you don't have control over it. Doing your best before God de-fines a successful stepmother (as well as remembering that *best* doesn't mean "perfect." So accept His grace and forgiveness for the times you've blown it!).

Successful stepmom. That's you.

Remember, from these stepmothers' hearts to yours: You are greatly loved! We started our stepmom journey looking to Joshua as a role model, and we'll end it the same way. In his farewell address to the leaders (that's you, stepmom), Joshua comforts them that "the LORD your God fights for you, just as he promised" (Joshua 23:10).

It's so good to know we are not alone. So good to know it isn't all up to us. So good to know we can rest in our God and His supply. And then Joshua reminds the leaders, "You know with all your heart and soul that not one of all the good promises the LORD your God gave you has failed" (verse 14).

Nor will He fail us. So relax, stepmom. You and your family are in good hands!

ACKNOWLEDGMENTS

Kathi

Great thanks go to Erin MacPherson, Cheri Gregory, and Susy Flory (AKA the Bad Moms Club), who kept me together through all of this.

Thanks to Amanda and Jeremy, who made me a stepmom. I am so grateful that God lets me get to be a part of your lives.

Justen and Kimberly: For being the best stepkids to my husband. Love you both.

Renee Swope, Michele Cushatt, and Crystal Paine: God bless each of you. So thankful. So, so thankful.

My team: Kim Nowlin, Angela Bouma, Wendy Doyle, Sherri Johnson, and Julie Johnson.

Thanks go to Brandy Bruce, Larry Weeden, and Christi Lynn. Thank you for your vision and talent.

Rachelle Gardner: You are a gift.

To our families: the Richersons, the Lipps, and the Dobsons. Thanks for giving us the best stories.

And finally to Roger: Thank you for trusting me with your kids. I love you even more because of what God has shown us through the tough years. All my love.

Carol

Jim Boley: For your constant faith and abiding love; for your unfailing humor, grace, and patience. "In the name of Christ, to the glory of God." You are my beloved.

Abby, Allison, and Andrea Boley: Being your mom is a joy beyond compare. Each of you is a beautiful answer to my prayers, and I couldn't be more proud of you. Thank you for being brave and letting me share some of our stories. I can't even begin to tell you how much you are loved.

Abby: A special thanks to you for opening your heart and finding room there for me. What a gift you are! I love you.

My parents, Dan and Jane Daniels: For their support, encouragement, and love. I could not have asked for better parents. My first—and lifelong—fans. I love them. I wish Daddy were here to see this.

My mother- and father-in-law, Judy and Ken Boley: Although no longer with us, their love and influence live on. They welcomed me into their family. I loved them then and I love them now.

My sister and my sisters- and brothers-in-love, Donna and Jim Staiger, Mary Ann and Jim Boone, and Margaret and Ed Bond: You have each blessed me in your own special way. I am grateful that we are family. You are loved.

My Tuesday's Children writers' group (and therapy cohort): Not only are you gifted writers; you are beautiful women and faithful friends. I'm thankful "We're Doing Life Together" (weredoinglife together.wordpress.com)—Linda Carlblom, Betty Arthurs, Judy Robertson, Donna Goodrich, Peggy Levesque, Jane Jimenez, Kitty Chappell, Andrea Huelsenbeck, Ashley Carlblom, Allison Boley, and Marsha Crockett.

My church family at Valley View Bible Church in Paradise Valley, Arizona: You are family to me in every sense of the word. I am so blessed by you, and I love you.

My professors and friends from the University of Arizona and Wheaton College: You have contributed to my life in so many ways, and I am grateful. Bear Down! Roll Thunder!

Rachelle Gardner, agent extraordinaire: Thank you for all of your hard work on this project. We couldn't have done it without you.

The team at Focus on the Family, especially Brandy Bruce, Larry Weeden, and Christi Lynn: You have a huge job to do, and you do it so well. Focus has been a part of our family for more than thirty years, and I am grateful. Your expertise blesses so many.

The team at Tyndale: Thank you for the faithful use of your gifts. The kingdom is advanced because of you.

Kathi Lipp: Thanks for saying yes to this whole idea. Thanks for telling me about the soles of your shoes melting to the tarmac in Phoenix. I knew then that we could be friends.

All the stepmoms who took the time to share their stories and their hearts with me: You are heroes in my eyes, and I am so proud of you. You are a blessing to your families and to me. Your stories and love will bless others as well. Carry on, my sisters. I love you.

Jesus Christ, King of Kings, Lord of Lords, Lover of my soul: It's all about You. Thank You for loving me and being so kind and gracious to me. I am grateful beyond words. I love You.

Notes

Introduction

1. US Census Bureau statistics, cited in Stepfamily Foundation, "Stepfamily Statistics," accessed October 4, 2014, http://www .stepfamily.org/stepfamily-statistics.html.
2. Data cited in Ron L. Deal, "A Call to Action: Reaction to the Pew Research Report," January 14, 2011, Smart Stepfamilies, www.smartstepfamilies.com/view/calltoaction.
3. Phil McGraw, *Family First* (New York: Free Press, 2004), 26.
4. James Dobson, *Complete Marriage and Family Home Reference Guide* (Carol Stream, IL: Tyndale House, 2000), 205.
5. Letter from C. S. Lewis to Sheldon Vanauken, April 22, 1953, quoted in Sheldon Vanauken, *A Severe Mercy* (New York: HarperCollins, 1980), 134.

Chapter 2

1. Henry Cloud and John Townsend, *God Will Make a Way* (Nashville: Integrity, 2003), 176.
2. Rick Warren, *The Purpose-Driven Life* (Grand Rapids: Zondervan, 2002), 196–97.

Chapter 3

1. Ron Deal, "Placing Your Spouse in the 'Front Seat' of Your Heart," FamilyLife.com, 2012, http://www.familylife.com /articles/topics/blended-family/remarriage/staying-married /placing-your-spouse-in-the-front-seat-of-your-heart#.U62 buvldWE8.

Chapter 5

1. Henry Cloud and John Townsend, *Boundaries with Kids* (Grand Rapids: Zondervan, 1998), 219.
2. Ibid., 99.
3. Gary Chapman, *The Five Love Languages of Teenagers* (Chicago: Northfield Publishing, 2005), 244.
4. Ron L. Deal, "Redeeming the Remarried," *Christianity Today*, October 10, 2007, 32.
5. Michael S. Moore, *Reconciliation: A Study of Biblical Families in Conflict* (Joplin, MO: College Press, 1994), 147.

Chapter 6

1. Beth Moore, *Get Out of That Pit* (Nashville: Integrity, 2007), 151.
2. Rick Warren, *The Purpose-Driven Life* (Grand Rapids: Zondervan, 2002), 17.
3. Kevin Leman, *Living in a Step-Family Without Getting Stepped On* (Nashville: Thomas Nelson, 1994), 235.
4. Gary Chapman, *The Five Love Languages* (Chicago: Northfield Publishing, 1995).
5. Gary Chapman, *The Five Love Languages of Teenagers* (Chicago: Northfield Publishing, 2005).
6. Gary Chapman and Ross Campbell, *The Five Love Languages of Children* (Chicago: Northfield Publishing, 1997).
7. Leman, *Living in a Step-Family Without Getting Stepped On*, 242.
8. Tony Campolo and Mary Albert Darling, *Connecting Like Jesus* (San Francisco: John Wiley & Sons, 2010), 118.
9. All material in this book quoted by Jennifer Cecil and Deborah Tyrrell is taken from interviews. Used by permission.

10. Charlie, quoted in Kitty Chappell, *Soaring Above the Ashes on the Wings of Forgiveness* (Mustang, OK: Tate Publishing, 2013), 241.

11. Charles Stanley, "From the Pastor's Heart" Newsletter, In Touch Ministries Daily Devotion, May 2013.

Chapter 8

1. Gary Smalley and Greg Smalley, *Bound by Honor: Fostering a Great Relationship with Your Teen* (Carol Stream, IL: Tyndale House, 1998), 14.

2. Ibid., 4.

3. Beth Moore, *So Long, Insecurity: You've Been a Bad Friend to Us* (Carol Stream, IL: Tyndale House, 2010), 115.

4. Dennis Rainey and Barbara Rainey, *Parenting Today's Adolescent* (Nashville: Thomas Nelson, 1998), 167.

5. Thomas K. Connellan, *Bringing Out the Best in Others!* (Austin, TX: Bard Press, 2003), 91.

6. Ibid., 92.

7. Chip Ingram, *Effective Parenting in a Defective World* (Carol Stream, IL: Tyndale House, 2006), 121.

8. Kathi Lipp, *The Husband Project* (Eugene, OR: Harvest House, 2009).

9. Henry Cloud and John Townsend, *12 "Christian" Beliefs That Can Drive You Crazy* (Grand Rapids: Zondervan, 1995), 16.

10. Caroline Leaf, *Who Switched Off My Brain? Controlling Toxic Thoughts and Emotions* (Southlake, TX: Inprov, 2009), 93.

11. Ibid., 95.

Chapter 10

1. *The Blues Brothers*, directed by John Landis (Universal Pictures, 1980).

2. *Gravity*, directed by Alfonso Cuarón (Warner Brothers, 2013).

3. Anne Graham Lotz, "Time Alone with Jesus," December 1 devotion, AnGeL Ministries, accessed October 5, 2014, http://www.annegrahamlotz.org/resources/daily-devotional/12/1/.

4. Stormie Omartian, *Lord, I Want to Be Whole* (Nashville: Thomas Nelson, 2000), 22.

5. Anne Ortlund, *Disciplines of the Beautiful Woman* (Waco, TX: Word Books, 1977), 29.

6. Woman quoted in Kevin Leman, *Living in a Step-Family Without Getting Stepped On* (Nashville: Thomas Nelson, 1994), 277.

7. Philip Yancey, *Prayer: Does It Make Any Difference?* (Grand Rapids: Zondervan, 2006), Kindle edition, emphasis added.

Chapter 12

1. Suzanne Eller, *The Unburdened Heart* (Ventura, CA: Regal, 2013), 148.

2. Dallas Demmitt and Nancy Demmitt, *Can You Hear Me Now?* (Colorado Springs: Cook Communications, 2003), 125.

3. Anne Graham Lotz, *Wounded by God's People: Discovering How God's Love Heals Our Hearts* (Grand Rapids: Zondervan, 2013), 200.

4. Kevin Huggins, *Parenting Adolescents* (Colorado Springs: NavPress, 1989), 231.

5. Ed Wimberly, "A Parent's Guide to Raising Great Kids," *Westmont College Magazine*, Summer 1999 issue, 23.

6. Inspector Sydney Wang, quoted in *Murder by Death*, directed by Robert Moore (Columbia Pictures, 1976).

7. Jodi Werhanowicz, quote taken from interview. Used by permission.

8. Eller, *The Unburdened Heart*, 174, 181.

FOCUS ON THE FAMILY®

Welcome to the Family —

Whether you purchased this book, borrowed it, or received it as a gift, thanks for reading it! This is just one of many insightful, biblically based resources that Focus on the Family produces for people in all stages of life.

Focus is a global Christian ministry dedicated to helping families thrive as they celebrate and cultivate God's design for marriage and experience the adventure of parenthood. Our outreach exists to support individuals and families in the joys and challenges they face, and to equip and empower them to be the best they can be.

Through our many media outlets, we offer help and hope, promote moral values and share the life-changing message of Jesus Christ with people around the world.

Focus on the Family MAGAZINES

These faith-building, character-developing publications address the interests, issues, concerns, and challenges faced by every member of your family from preschool through the senior years.

For More INFORMATION

ONLINE:
Log on to
FocusOnTheFamily.com
In Canada, log on to
FocusOnTheFamily.ca

PHONE:
Call toll-free:
800-A-FAMILY
(232-6459)
In Canada, call toll-free:
800-661-9800

THRIVING FAMILY®
Marriage & Parenting

FOCUS ON THE FAMILY CLUBHOUSE JR.®
Ages 4 to 8

FOCUS ON THE FAMILY CLUBHOUSE®
Ages 8 to 12

FOCUS ON THE FAMILY CITIZEN®
U.S. news issues

Rev. 3/11

Meet the rest of the family

Expert advice on parenting and marriage . . .
spiritual growth . . . powerful personal stories . . .

Focus on the Family's collection of inspiring, practical resources can help your family grow closer to God—and each other—than ever before. Whichever format you need—video, audio, book or eBook—we have something for you. Visit our online Family Store and discover how we can help your family thrive at **FocusOnTheFamily.com/resources**.